PHILOSOPHY
of HAPPINESS

The Key to Heaven on Earth

ART CORPUS

Philosophy of Happiness

Copyright © [2024] by **Art Corpus**

For permissions requests, contact:

Writersway Solutions, LLC

4833 Glendale Avenue

Glendale, CA 91204

www.writerswaysolutions.com

1-888-666-4258

ISBN (Paperback): 978-1-96273-323-6

ISBN (Ebook): 978-1-96273-324-3

Printed in the United States of America

CONTENTS

PREFACE

Happiness is the most elusive goal of human existence and, maybe for that reason, the most sought after. That qualifies it to be the understatement not only of the year but of all times. The first cry of a newborn child is an irresistible demand for happiness. The last breath of a dying person is a silent plea for happiness. In between those two extremes are innumerable sighs, laughter, moans, smiles, groans, and other human behaviors that spell happiness or lack of it. Indeed, the whole spectrum of human life bespeaks of the various colors of man's unending desire for happiness. In short, happiness is the summum bonum (highest good) of human existence.

Hence, whether we realize it or not, everything we do is colored by our desire for happiness. In other words, all our actions are motivated by happiness.

But why is happiness that important for humans? Is there nothing better or superior goal in life than happiness? Is the salvation of one's soul—as taught by religion—not a better option? Or Buddhahood perhaps? Or even the sublime and enduring love aspired by the romantics? Or to be more down to earth, the colossal power sought after by politicians or the vast, enormous wealth the ambitious businessman is dying for? Is not any of these or all these more valuable or more desirable and, therefore, worth dying or living for than the elusive goal called happiness?

A cogent evaluation of the human situation vis-à-vis the conundrum called happiness should give a negative answer. All who aspire for any or all these human goals do so only for one reason: happiness. They think that at the end of the rainbow of any or all these endeavors, they will find the pot of gold in the form of happiness—only to be disappointed again and again. That is how invasive and elusive this virus called happiness is. It is worse than an airborne disease. It is transmitted by means of agencies humans do not even suspect. It has entered all the nooks and crannies of human existence. It has infiltrated all the dimensions of human life. Everything we do is done in the guise of happiness. People commit crimes, harm themselves and others, and do all sorts of abominations in the guise of happiness. Whether Freud realized it or not, happiness is the foundation and rationale of his theory with the moniker "pleasure principle."

Thus, it goes without saying that happiness is the ultimate goal of human life and existence. And unless and until this goal is reached, there will always be in man's being, a huge natural vacuum demanding to be filled in accordance with the principle that nature abhors vacuum. And it goes without saying that unless and until this vacuum is filled, there will be no peace in man's soul. And it also goes without saying, that unless and until there will be peace in man's soul, there will be no peace on earth.

Peace has always been my lifetime obsession; I do not know why. Perhaps, it is because I was born and grew up in a warring family. My parents, even when they were in their sixties and therefore should have settled all their differences, were still behaving like cats and dogs— maybe even worse. My four siblings and myself were always at each other's throat. Peace in the family was a rare delicacy and came like a blue moon. I have this theory that we were enemies in our previous lives and karma brought us together in one family to be reconciled. But it did not happen. Perhaps our relationship in this life is worse than before. I just wonder what it will be in our next life.

Thus, I have had more than enough of war in my life—just in the confines of a small family. But what about out there in the whole wide world? It is a fearsome world of unspeakable violence since the beginning of time. The so-called holy book, the Bible—which religion calls the word of God—started the story of man with the story of Adam and Eve, a story of a mini-war between God and man. This was followed by a story of deadly violence between brothers, Cain and Abel, the story of the first fratricide. Then came a more violent story, the story of the Great Flood unleashed by a wrathful God decimating not only sinful humans but even innocent plants and animals. Next in the agenda of a cruel God was the horrible fate of Sodom and Gomorrah on whose hapless people God rained fire and brimstones. And on and on and on. The Bible, this so-called holy book, never tired of telling endless stories of violence. It is beyond my comprehension why the Bible is called the word of God and why the cruel biblical God who loves to feast on blood, death, and violence is called God. I do not know about others, but I have long disowned the horrible, dreadful, and monstrous biblical God who loves war. My personal God is a God of love and peace.

But what about the story of humans outside the Bible? It is definitely a story of man's cruelty to man as shown by the loathsome Inquisition and Crusade, by the endless wars between the so-called civilized nations in Europe, by two genocidal world wars, by the unspeakably horrendous holocaust, and on and on. Indeed, the litany of human madness is endless. As I am writing this book to promote peace, there is a war going on in Gaza between the Hamas and the Israelites, a war in Afghanistan, in Iraq, and in Syria where ISIS, a Muslim organization is in a deadly rampage of extermination against their fellow Muslims.

All these wars, all this deadly violence of man's inhumanity to man, make my head spin in confusion, my stomach sour in disgust, and my head torn in anguish. I hate war! I hate violence! My whole being cries out for peace! But there is no peace! What to do then? Shall I go to the Himalayas, find a cave, and hole up myself there? Shall I then find peace? But what about the rest of the world? Can I find peace while the whole world is at war? Can I be happy while the whole of humanity is suffering?

My answer to these questions is in this book. And this book gives a simple answer: there can be no peace without happiness. There can be no peace in the world if there is no peace in men's soul because the world is a mere reflection of the state of men's soul. And there can be no peace in men's soul if there is no happiness therein. The answer is indeed simple. But as you go on reading this book, you will know that the answer is not really that simple. Nevertheless, simple or not, you have to know the answer yourself so you can find happiness and peace in your own life. And if you multiply yourself sufficiently, there will be peace on earth—finally. And happiness too.

And so, read on.

INTRODUCTION

Pure hubris! These are maybe the two best words you can think of to describe this book—after reading it, of course. And so, go ahead and read it. And be appalled. And be entertained. And finally, be enlightened.

Be appalled at the temerity of an unknown author trying to unravel the intellectual Gordian knot that happiness is—an undertaking which befuddled even the brilliant mind of the greatest philosopher of all times, Aristotle,1 and the greatest theologian the Catholic Church has produced, Thomas Aquinas. Indeed, happiness is a subject which, as the pundit says, even angels fear to tread.

Be entertained at the intellectual magic the author conjured to prove his amazing thesis, tricks that are actually as simple as boiling an egg or making an instant coffee.

And finally, be enlightened that this seemingly intellectual thaumaturgy is, after all, the correct recipe, the right formula, if you will, to achieve human happiness and, eventually, to change the world by ushering peace—a feat which everybody wants to do but cannot even begin to start doing.

This sui generis book is a long-awaited fulfillment of a promise I made in my previous books on human health2 and human sexuality.3 It is a promise that in a subsequent book, I will eventually provide the reader and the whole world the real and ultimate solution to the perennial problem of humans that prevents the coming of peace on earth. That problem is so all encompassing that it includes human problems on health and even sexuality.

To be sure, there are different perspectives regarding the real ultimate problem of humans. There is the perspective of Buddha who saw that the ultimate human problem is suffering. The solution he offered, therefore, is to end this suffering by eliminating the perceived cause which is desire rooted in human ego. He reasoned out that since the cause of human suffering is unfulfilled human desires, eliminate human desires, and thus, suffering, its effect, will thereby be eliminated. His logic seems valid enough. His premise that the cause of human suffering is unfulfilled human desires rooted in human ego conforms with the reality of human experience. However, his conclusion that the solution therefore is to eliminate human desires and suffering will also be eliminated is dubious and does not square with the reality of the human situation. No wonder his laudable mission eventually failed, and Buddhism became, at best, an esoteric religion. But one cannot really blame Buddha. He was a wonderful mystic but a poor philosopher. He was relatively young4 when he embarked on his quixotic mission to end human suffering. Having been kept in the confines of his father's palace, he was deprived of the necessary experience to have a rational grasp of the human situation and a realistic understanding of human nature. He was misled by his blissful mystical experiences during his meditations in which human desire no longer plays a role and practically does not exist. So he thought that if other humans could experience what he did, there would be an end to human suffering. In that sense, he was right. But he was wrong in thinking that every human is like him and can be like him, a mystic. Unfortunately, he failed to see that there is an alternative to the solution of human suffering, one that is realistic and doable by all humans regardless of their spiritual stature. That solution is the thesis of this book—as you will find out shortly.

Another perspective regarding the solution to the ultimate problem of humans is that offered by Jesus Christ who came after Buddha. Buddha and Christ are in the opposite ends of the human spectrum regarding happiness. Whereas Buddha promised human happiness in this life, Christ promised human salvation after this life, in another unknown life which Christians call heaven, the nature of which nobody knows—not even Christ himself, it seems, since he only spoke of it vaguely as "my [his] father's kingdom." Whereas Buddha is a natural (not religious) mystic and a down-to-earth but still wet-in-the-ear philosopher, but a philosopher nevertheless, Christ is a religious fanatic and a miracle worker. Indeed, no two individuals can be as opposite as Buddha and Christ. Nevertheless, they have something in common: their burning love for their fellow humans, love that inspired them both to attempt to end human suffering albeit, again, their formulas are as opposite as earth and heaven.

Since Christ was no scientist nor a philosopher but a religious teacher, his formula is not a formula at all. His teachings, as found in the canonical Gospels, can best be described as a syncretism culled from the major religions prevailing during his time, namely Judaism and Hinduism. His teachings, to be sure, are exceptionally wonderful, to say the least, so much so that even today, they are often the topics of Church's sermons and the subject of religious epistles. His pronouncements: love your enemies, do good to those who hate you; if somebody slaps you, turn the other cheek; he who has no sin cast the first stone; give to Caesar what belongs to Caesar and to God what belongs to God; the Sabbath is made for man, not man for the Sabbath; be ye perfect as the heavenly Father is perfect—to mention just a few—have no equal in ethical grandeur and idealism. The problem is, they are just that: ethical idealism—far removed from the concrete reality of human existence. Therefore, these teachings of his, no matter how wonderful, cannot be put into practice in our daily life because it has to take a perfect man to be able to execute them. But where can we find a perfect man? Who can be perfect as God is perfect?

Even Jesus Christ, as the Gospels picture him, is far from being perfect. As a young man, he does not give a damn about hurting the feelings of his parents when he got "lost" for three days without telling them of his whereabouts—on the pretext of being "about my [his] Father's business" (Luke 3:42–49). He is cruel when he gets mad. As the Gospel says: "And he found in the temple those who sold oxen and sheep and doves, and the money changers doing business. When he had made a whip of cords, He drove them all out of the Temple, with the sheep and the oxen, and poured out the changers' money and overturned the tables" (John 2:14–15; Mark 11:15). Nay, Christ even cursed to death a poor fig tree when he could not find fruit there because, as the Gospel says, "it was not the season for figs"5 (Mark 11:13–14; Matthew 29:18–20). These biblical incidents clearly show Christ not only as an imperfect man but even as a cruel and a stupid one. If Christ himself could not practice what he preached, how could ordinary mortals like us follow his footsteps?

Christ's perspective of solving the ultimate problem of man is, therefore, essentially flawed, to say the least. He expects imperfect humans to behave in a perfect way: a classic case of putting the cart before the horse, so to speak. And worse, he tells people to be perfect without telling them how to do it. No wonder we humans who are enamored with Christ cannot move forward. No wonder Christ, like Buddha, was a failure. In modern idiom, they are both losers.

From the mistakes and failures of Buddha and Christ, the foremost giants in the realm of ethics and spirituality, there is definitely a huge lesson to be learned. That lesson is found in the following pages of this book.

Read on.

1

Mainstream Philosophy on Happiness

Valiant attempts have been made by various philosophers to unravel the conundrum nature of happiness. These attempts throughout the ages started, as far as recorded history can show, from the Grecian past to the present. These attempts, no matter how valiant, have produced nothing more than an interesting intellectual chiaroscuro of diversities of views caused, no doubt, not by the nature of the subject but by the understandable differences of personal viewpoints on the subject. This phenomenon reminds me of the age-old story of the elephant and the five blind men who have different perceptions of the elephant depending of which part of the elephant they have touched. Hence, there are as many philosophical views on happiness as there are philosophers. Moreover, not all philosophers are interested in happiness. Many of them are more in love with esoteric subjects like metaphysics, epistemology, mathematics, and the like, than with happiness. Fortunately for us, however, quite a few of the outstanding ones, like Socrates, Plato, and Aristotle, had the wisdom to spend some of their awesome intellectual energy on this mundane but momentous subject. Thus, they made the world intellectually richer, if not a better place to live in.

You and I, therefore, will walk through the salient thoughts of these brilliant philosophers of different times and climes not only for our personal erudition but more importantly for our much needed enlightenment on this crucial matter.

We start from Greece, the cradle of western philosophy and home to the most brilliant minds of humanity, and walk with the most controversial and colorful personality of them all: Socrates.

Socrates[6]

Socrates not only lived his philosophy to the full. He also died for it—willingly—by drinking the deadly hemlock. In that sense, he is in the same league with his kindred spirit, Jesus Christ, who also died for his principles. Socrates was born in Athens in 460 BCE. A thoroughbred iconoclast, Socrates impugned the prevailing view of his fellow Athenians that happiness was a rare commodity, a special gift of the gods for their chosen ones. He argued that happiness was for everybody since it could be obtained through human efforts. Although he has not written anything, the mighty pen of his most outstanding student, Plato, has recorded the following ideas of Socrates on happiness which we have culled from the internet at www.PursuitofHappiness.org. They are the following:

Plato[7]

1. All humans naturally desire happiness.
2. Happiness is obtainable through human efforts.
3. Happiness depends not on external goods but on how humans use them.
4. Happiness depends on one's success in harmonizing his conflicting desires toward the pursuit of knowledge and virtue from which one can derive real happiness.
5. Virtue is an essential ingredient of happiness and vice versa.

Plato is another outstanding brilliant philosopher the world has ever known. Like his teacher Socrates, he was born and lived in Athens. He founded in Athens the famous Academy, a school of philosophy where Aristotle, his most brilliant student, had his education. He recorded his philosophical thoughts in what is now known as the *Dialogues of Plato*. In *The Republic*, arguably his most outstanding opus in which he unraveled his ideas of an ideal republic, Plato wrote his thoughts on happiness which are summarized as follows:

1. Happiness is the equilibrium state of the three parts of the soul, viz., reason, will, and desire.
2. Happiness which is permanent is not pleasure which is temporary.
3. The pursuit of happiness should be made by the use of our reason; otherwise, failure will result.
4. The pursuit of fleeting pleasures and self-aggrandizement is not rational.
5. The experience of the "beautiful" will free us from our slavery to fleeting pleasures and self-aggrandizement.

Aristotle[8]

The Philosopher, as Thomas Aquinas called Aristotle, has the most impressive curriculum vitae of all philosophers. Aside from being the most brilliant of Plato's student in the Academy, he was also a founder of his own school, the Lyceum, the first scientific institution of learning which rivaled the Academy in excellence and popularity. His reputation as a most outstanding teacher no doubt influenced to a great degree the decision of King Philip of Macedon to make Aristotle the tutor of his son, Alexander, who eventually became Alexander the Great, one of the greatest conquerors of all times.

Aristotle's awesome prodigious talents embrace not only philosophy but also mathematics, physics, biology, botany, agriculture, medicine, politics, ethics, and aesthetics among others. As a pioneer in logic, his name is indelibly associated with it as Aristotelian logic. Eudaemonia, his term for happiness in his celebrated opus, *Nicomachean Ethics* is a byword in the academe. His philosophy on happiness is summarized as follows:

1. Happiness is the summum bonum (highest good) of human life.
2. Happiness is neither pleasure nor virtue but the exercise of virtue.
3. The entire life of a person is the measure of his happiness.
4. Virtuous friendship is of the highest kind and most important in achieving happiness.
5. Virtue, which is essential for happiness, is the golden mean between the extremes of excess and deficiency.
6. Happiness consists of a lifetime of possession of all the goods that lead to the perfection of human nature and enrichment of human life.

Epicurus[9]

Of all philosophers, only Epicurus has a name synonymous with pleasure. An epicure is one who seeks pleasure, not just the ordinary commonplace pleasure but the kind sought after by one who has a sensitive and discriminating taste. Indeed, Epicurus was an epicure par excellence—and much, much more. For Epicurus, the most pleasant and pleasurable life is one characterized by inner tranquility (ataraxia) amidst a pleasure garden of beautiful natural surrounding among friends and students discussing philosophy while listening to the soft music of a lyre. Pleasure, therefore, for Epicurus is not the crass hedonism characterized by gross revelry over food, drink, and sex, but the exquisite pleasure caused by inner tranquility (absence of pain and worry), contentment with simple things in life among friends of kindred spirit sharing the esoteric pleasure of philosophical thoughts.

Graphically, Epicurus's ideas of happiness are the following:

1. Happiness is pleasure: the simple, exquisite, noble, refined, and natural things in life.
2. Happiness is freedom from bodily pains and that of the mind (worry)—in short, inner tranquility (ataraxia).
3. Happiness is a life among friends (kindred spirit) in the common pursuit of wisdom and true happiness.

Buddha[10]

Buddha was an atheist in the sense that his philosophy has nothing to do with God or religion. This is especially true with regard to his philosophy on happiness. For Buddha, happiness is not grounded in God nor does it depend on God in any way. Happiness consists basically in the understanding of the root causes of suffering in this life. To understand this philosophy—a very unique one, indeed — you have to know Buddha's life and how he came to embrace such a philosophy which attracted and became the guiding star of so many lives.

Buddha was born Prince Siddhartha Gautama circa early century BCE in a place which is now the modern-day Nepal. He was born to a wealthy royal family where he was raised in worldly luxury and deprived of the experience of suffering. However, out of curiosity, perhaps, he escaped one day from his golden cage and explored the outside world where he encountered an old man, a sick man, and a dead man. He also met an ascetic yet happy monk. This extreme experience provided the impetus and the rationale for his quest to end human suffering—propelled, no doubt, by an overwhelming feeling of supreme compassion for mankind. The rest of the story you already know: how he left his family, lived an extremely ascetic life, and finally found enlightenment while meditating under a bodhi tree.

Buddha's philosophy to end human suffering and thus attain happiness is simplicity itself. It consists of the recognition of the causes of suffering (the Four Noble Truths) and their solution (the Eightfold Path)

The Four Noble Truths are:

1. Life is suffering (dukkha).
2. Suffering arises from desire.
3. Desire can be eliminated.
4. Elimination of desire results from following the right way (the Eightfold Path).

The Eightfold Path are:

1. Right understanding
2. Right intention
3. Right speech
4. Right action
5. Right livelihood
6. Right effort
7. Right mindfulness
8. Right concentration

The Eightfold Path can be classified as follows: 1 and 2 refer to wisdom, 3–5 to ethical conduct, and 6–8 to mental cultivation.

This is not the proper forum (because of lack of time and space) for a thorough discussion of Buddha's philosophy regarding happiness in terms of the Four Noble Truths and the Eightfold Path. It is quite obvious that an understanding of this magnitude will require the writing of another book. Suffice it to say that the bottom line of Buddha's philosophy on happiness consists of achieving a state of mind detached from all the needs and wants of life and thereby achieve a state of permanent bliss (nirvana).

Thomas Aquinas[11]

If Buddha was a prince of India, Aquinas was a prince of the Catholic Church. Buddha had such a magnificent mind that he earned the moniker "Buddha" (the enlightened one), while Aquinas had such a colossal intellect that he was called angelic doctor of the Catholic Church. They both renounced their noble, wealthy life and lived a spiritual life. But the similarities between the two end there. Buddha and Aquinas belong to the opposite ends of human spectrum. Buddha was an itinerant preacher who had to beg for his food while Aquinas was a cloistered Dominican monk whose needs were well provided for by the wealthy religious order. Buddha was a married man while Aquinas was a celibate monk. Buddha's philosophy is bereft of any idea of God, while Aquinas's is saturated with and grounded in theology. Buddha taught that perfect happiness (nirvana) is attainable in this life, while Aquinas taught that perfect happiness (beatitude) can be found only after life.

Thomas Aquinas was an Italian noble born in Naples to a wealthy aristocratic family. Eventually, he renounced his nobility and wealth and became a monk. The story goes that when he was a student of Albertus Magnus (Albert the Great), he was given by his classmates the name Dumb Ox for his being silent in class and for his egregious corpulence. He was a prolific writer. He produced some forty books including his magna opera, *Summa Theologiae* (Summary of Theology) and *Summa Contra Gentiles* (Summary of Doctrines Against the Gentiles) wherein he delved into the issue of human happiness which he defined as the summum bonum. Thus, he wrote in *Summa Theologiae*: "It is impossible for any created good to constitute man's happiness. For happiness is that perfect good which entirely satisfies one's desire; otherwise it will not be the ultimate end, if something yet remained to be desired. Now, the object of the will, i.e., of man's desire, is what is universally good; just as the object of the intellect is what is universally true. Hence, it is evident that nothing can satisfy man's will except what is universally good. This is to be found not in any creature, but in God alone, because every creature has only participated goodness. Therefore, God alone can satisfy the will of man according to the words of the Psalm (102:5), 'who alone satisfies your desire with good things.' Therefore, God alone constitutes man's happiness."[12]

In short, happiness for Aquinas is the satisfaction of human desires that only God can satisfy. The next chapter will show that this is not a realistic definition of happiness but an idealistic one which, needless to say, cannot be proven and beyond the ambit of philosophy.

Jesus of Nazareth

This man needs no introduction. Of all members of the human race, Jesus is the most controversial and, therefore, the most popular. Indeed, he is the epitome of contradiction. People celebrate his birthday on the vernal equinox. And yet nobody knows exactly when he was born. People say that he was born in Bethlehem. And yet some say that he lives only in the legendary world, that he is a fiction of history. Others say that he is a Christian imitation of the Roman god Mithra whose life mirrors that of Christ or the other way around. Truly, the litany of the contradictions that surround the persona of Jesus of Nazareth is endless. Nevertheless, since innumerable lives are impacted—for good or evil—by his very name since the very dawn of history, we have no choice but to include him among the list of those remarkable personages that made a difference in the lives of humans in terms of happiness. For the sake of simplicity, we shall limit our discussion within the pages of the four canonical Gospels that are arguably the best evidence of his existence, life, and teachings.

The Gospel according to Matthew, the first canonical gospel, records the following first words of Jesus that strongly suggest his thoughts regarding what happiness should be: "Man shall not live by bread alone but by every word that proceeds from the mouth of God" (Matthew 4:4). No doubt, these words imply that man's happiness consists not only in the fulfillment of his bodily needs but also of the needs of his spirit. And within the context of his having fasted for forty days and forty nights (Matthew 4:2), these words deliver the clear message that for Jesus, the needs of the spirit are more important than the needs of the body. (Our view on the matter is that the needs of the spirit and the body are equally important.) Matthew's gospel also records the first ever Sermon on the Mount delivered by Jesus in which he repeated the same spiritual theme regarding happiness, which is now known as the beatitude: "Blessed are the poor in spirit, for theirs is the kingdom of heaven. Blessed are those who mourn for they shall be comforted. Blessed are the meek, for they shall inherit the earth. Blessed are those who hunger and thirst for righteousness, for they shall be filled. Blessed are the merciful, for they shall obtain mercy. Blessed are the pure in heart, for they shall see God. Blessed are the peacemakers, for they shall be called sons of God. Blessed are those who are persecuted for righteousness sake, for theirs is the kingdom of God" (Matthew 5:3– 10). These beatitudes clearly show Jesus's partiality to spiritual matters when it comes to happiness. And this attitude of his is underscored in no uncertain terms when he said: "Therefore do not worry, saying, 'What shall we eat?' or 'What shall we drink?' or 'What shall we wear?'…But seek first the kingdom of God and His righteousness and all these things shall be added to you" (Matthew 6:31–33).

Indeed, seeking the kingdom of God is the major theme which dominates Jesus's life. And his life clearly shows that he found the kingdom of God in actively helping people by feeding their minds with his teachings, by feeding their body with food by performing miracles of multiplication of bread and fish, by performing numerous miracles of curing their various ailments, and other wonderful examples showing in no uncertain terms his overwhelming love for his fellow men, examples that embellish the pages of the gospels and showing to all and sundry the meaning in concrete examples of the kingdom of God.

Al-Ghazali[13]

Abu-Hamad al-Ghazali (1058–1111 CE) is an outstanding Islamic philosopher and theologian. Because of his exemplary life and outstanding intellect, he was appointed professor of theology at the University of Baghdad at the age of thirty-three. He was the supreme Islamic theologian of his time. Despite his success, he did not stay long in the academe. He had to answer the call of spirit beckoning him to a world of great spiritual grandeur. He left Baghdad to live with the Sufi monks in Syria. Then he went to Mecca for the

hadj, and there, he discovered his vocation to transform Islam from a religion of outward obedience to rules to a religion steeped in the interior life of the spirit.

Al-Ghazali wrote prodigiously about happiness. From his writings, we can glean the following salient points:

1. There is in every man an "inner pain" which demands to be relieved by happiness.
2. The primary step to happiness is to realize that one is a spiritual being.
3. The ultimate happiness is to experience one's identity with the ultimate reality.

Sigmund Freud[14]

This *rara avis* also needs no introduction. I am sure you know him well. People are so familiar with him because he is associated with sex, and sex is, of course, a popular commodity. To be sure, Freud's psychoanalytic philosophy revolves around sex. However, unknown to many, Freud is also a proponent of happiness. But of course, true to his character, his philosophy on happiness is strongly flavored with sex.

Freud defines happiness as the fulfillment of man's erotic instinct. Unfortunately for man, he himself prevents himself from being happy because he has created for his own protection an environment (society) which denies him the full expression of his erotic instinct. Society says that man may enjoy sexual expression only with the opposite sex and under certain conditions like marriage, among others. But man's erotic instinct does not recognize any condition. It demands expression with anyone it pleases, however it pleases, whenever it pleases, and wherever it pleases. This is the sad paradox of life, according to Freud.

As a compromise, man does one of two things: either he indulges his erotic instinct in secret or he represses it. Of course, those who do not want to compromise and brave enough (or perhaps foolhardy enough) to thumb their noses on society's norms simply indulge their erotic proclivities openly. Freud's theory of psychoanalysis deals exclusively with the phenomenon of repression of man's erotic desires. Since sex is energy, like any other form of energy, it may be transformed or channeled but not repressed. Since repression is basically suppression, it results in psychological aberrations like hysteria, the most common symptom of repression. It is to Freud's eternal credit that he devised psychoanalysis as an effective way of addressing this human problem which religion used to denounce as work of the devil.

According to Freud, this is where Christianity encountered its biggest stumbling block. By prescribing God as the only source of happiness, Christianity unwittingly puts in quandary and great psychological jeopardy those poor deluded souls who pursue God but, in the process, failed to find happiness. Freud's prophetic words are now realized in the cases of priests and ministers of religion who are not only having problems with their own sex lives but also giving these same problems to others—all because they suppress their sexual instinct in violation of natural law.

John Locke[15]

John Locke (1632–1704) is an English empiricist famously known for his epistemological theory that the human mind is originally a tabula rasa (blank slate) and that throughout a man's life, this blank slate is eventually filled up with knowledge derived from sensory experience. Unknown to many, he coined the phrase "pursuit of happiness" in his monumental opus, *An Essay Concerning Human Understanding*. Eventually, this phrase found its way in the US Declaration of Independence when Thomas Jefferson wrote that people have an "inalienable right to life, liberty, and pursuit of happiness."

A unique contribution of Locke to philosophy is the principle that pursuit of happiness is the basis and foundation of liberty since the former severs a person's bond of attachment to a particular perceived object of happiness and gives him the liberty to choose from different options and, ultimately, to decide on one that should redound to his best interest. The US Declaration of Independence should, therefore, be seen in this philosophical light provided by John Locke.

Locke, to his everlasting credit, also made an essential and existential connection between pursuit of happiness and political liberty which should be the guiding principle of all governments all over the world. He said that since the right to the pursuit of happiness is an inalienable right of everybody, which is limited only by the exercise of the same right by others, no government is justified in curtailing and controlling that right as long as it does not conflict with the exercise of the same right by others.

Aside from his views on happiness vis-à-vis individual and political liberty, Locke has also the following take on happiness, namely:

1. Happiness is essentially pleasure and unhappiness, pain.
2. It is important not to mistake "false pleasure" from "genuine pleasure." The former is fleeting and illusory. The latter is permanent and conducive to well-being.

Immanuel Kant[16]

Immanuel Kant (1724–1804) is one of the greatest, if not the greatest, German philosophers. Kant's major philosophical concern is ethics. His famous ethical principle, categorical imperative, which is equivalent to the Golden Rule, is a byword in the world of ethics. Although the idea of happiness plays a very minor role in his ethical and philosophical concern, still, his account of happiness is sufficient to unravel his thinking and position on this matter.

In his opus, *The Metaphysical Principles of Virtue*, Kant describes happiness in this fashion: "a continuous well-being, enjoyment of life, complete satisfaction with one's condition." In the same opus, Kant defines happiness as "getting what one's wants." In his *Critique of Practical Reason*, he expanded this definition as "the state of rational being in the world in the whole of his existence where everything goes according to his wish and will."

Since it is difficult to know what a rational being really "wish and will," happiness is really such a vague concept that made Kant conclude in his former opus that "happiness is not an ideal of reason but of imagination." This inevitably led Kant to conclude that the pursuit of happiness is futile and will not result in the acquisition of happiness. In other words, for Kant, nobody can be happy in this world. This might be an offshoot of his serious adherence to Christian teachings. Kant was a devoted Lutheran Christian.

William James[17]

William James (1842–1910) was an American philosopher. He was born in New York City on January 11, 1842. He was of Scot-Irish stock. He was the oldest of the five children of Henry James, a theologian of unusual intellectual and literally ability which was inherited by his son, the novelist Henry James Jr. Despite his weak eyes and periodic ill health, William James graduated with a degree of Doctor of Medicine at Harvard where he spent thirty-five years of his life teaching physiology, philosophy, and psychology until he retired in 1907 at the age of sixty-five. He was married with five children.

James lived at a time in the history of the world when the perennial struggle in the human mind between the forces of religion and materialism was most pronounced. James became a victim of this cultural malaise. He developed a severe depression which he described as a "crisis in meaning." However, he was able to get out of this crisis by a sheer act of free will. His experience colored to a considerable degree his philosophical standpoint regarding happiness. The salient points of his views on happiness are as follows:

1. Happiness is a result of an existential choice to actively participate in the game of life.

2. Happiness comes with the courage to face the unknown dimensions of life by taking courageous acts of faith in dealing with the uncertainties of daily life.

3. Happiness is a free and meaningful life, not as a result of rational convictions but of simply going through life with the conviction that life is free and meaningful. Hence, happiness is a product—not of a rational act but of an act of the will.

John Dewey[18]

John Dewey (1859–1952) was also an American philosopher. He was born on October 20, 1859, in Burlington, Vermont. He finished his undergraduate studies majoring in philosophy at the University of Vermont. Subsequently, he studied at the Johns Hopkins University where he acquired his doctorate degree in philosophy. Like William James, he spent most of his productive life in the academia teaching at the University of Michigan, then at the University of Chicago, and lastly at the Columbia University. Like James, he was also a family man with several children.

Dewey's fame arose from his being an educator par excellence rather than from his life's other achievements. His philosophy on education is deeply rooted in the novel idea of "learning by doing," a proactive approach which is diametrically opposed to the prevailing method of his time which was "passive learning" by listening to lectures and passing examinations to earn grades, an educational approach which still prevails in the present educational systems of the world.

Thus, Dewey's novel philosophy on education spawned understandably a slew of controversy. Notwithstanding, he stuck to his pragmatic approach which he encapsulated in these words written in his "My Pedagogic Creed": "I believe that the school must represent present life—life as real and vital to the child as that which he carries on in the home, in the neighborhood, or in the playground."

Dewey's philosophy on happiness is powerfully expressed in these powerful words: "To find out what one is fitted to do and to secure an opportunity to do it is the key to happiness. Such happiness as life is capable of comes from the full participation of all our powers in the endeavor to wrest from each changing situations of experience its own full and unique meaning."

In short, happiness for Dewey consists of finding your true vocation in life and living it fully. It is a philosophy of happiness which mirrors his own life.

Chapter

2

The Nature of Happiness

This is the core of the thesis of this book: the essence or nature of happiness. Just as we cannot find something unless we know what we are looking for, so also, we cannot find happiness unless we know what happiness is, what really is the nature of this elusive goal of human life. That is the problem of defining happiness: its elusive nature. As we have seen from the previous chapter, there are as many definitions of happiness as there are people who seek to define it. Out of curiosity, I look to see how *Merriam-Webster* fares in defining it, and as I suspected, the dictionary is more in the dark on this subject than I. According to it, happiness is this, and I quote verbatim: "1. Obs. Good fortune: PROSPERITY. 2a: a state of well-being and contentment; JOY b: a pleasurable or satisfying experience 3: FELICITY, APTNESS." At first blush, these definitions seem satisfactory. However, a more cogent analysis will show that none of these really defines happiness. They are merely the effects or the results or the by-products of happiness but not happiness itself. They are indeed—all of them—desirable, but how do we acquire them if we do not know their ultimate cause which is happiness? Obviously, the lexicographer is not a philosopher. Well, the job of a lexicographer is difficult enough. It would be asking too much to include in that precious skill the abstruse talent of a philosopher. Let us therefore leave *Webster* alone and continue our task of unravelling the nature of happiness.

Actually, *Webster* has already given us the clue to the answer to this most difficult question which baffled even the brilliant minds of the philosophers and religious leaders we mentioned in the previous chapter. All the words *Webster* used to define happiness, such as joy, contentment, state of well-being, felicity, etc., have one thing in common, i.e., they describe a state of being which is the result or effect of the fulfillment or satisfaction of human needs. In other words, they are the results or effects of happiness. Therefore, happiness is simply the fulfillment or satisfaction of human needs. Let me repeat that: happiness is the fulfillment or satisfaction of human needs. Note well that this definition is unlike all the other definitions of happiness that describe the effects of happiness. To use an analogy in physics, happiness is a vacuum in human needs filled.

I know you find this simple definition of happiness a kind of a letdown, if not altogether simplistic. I know you are expecting a more abstruse and complicated definition befitting philosophy. This is one of the numerous paradoxes in life: the simplest things are the ones that seem most complicated. This is also a common misconception. My brand of philosophy, however, is simplicity and clarity in consonance with my philosophy that philosophy should be a beacon in the dark night of human life. However, some, if not most, so-called philosophers, as the likes of Wittgenstein and his kindred spirits, erroneously think that to be profound is to be abstruse and complicated to the misery of students of philosophy. On the contrary, the truth is, as previously mentioned, the real task of a genuine philosopher is to unravel reality which is complicated enough. To make it more complicated is to totally miss the point and exacerbate the problem. The real challenge of a philosopher worth his salt is to simplify and clarify what is complicated and difficult such that it can be understood by anybody—even by a young boy or girl with ordinary intelligence. If a philosopher cannot do that, then he is not worthy of the name.

After that lengthy digression, let me now go back to our subject. We humans, like other creatures, have many needs. Everybody knows this. These needs are literally vacuums demanding to be filled in consonance with the natural law we learned in physics that nature abhors vacuum, as exemplified by the gadget siphon and the natural phenomenon of lightning and thunder. In both of these examples, a vacuum is made, which nature immediately filled thereby creating the flow of liquid in the siphon and the sound of thunder. Since nature abhors vacuum and human needs are really vacuums, nature will do anything and everything and will not rest until these vacuums are filled. Nature's attempt to eliminate these vacuums naturally create tension, stress, strain, and other unpleasant feelings or emotions that naturally make humans unhappy so that they will do everything they can to eliminate them. But since the only way to do this is to satisfy these needs or to fill up these vacuums resulting in pleasant feelings or emotions, this satisfaction of needs, this elimination of abhorrent vacuums, is this not the essence of happiness? It surely is.

To further elucidate this natural dynamics of happiness, let us take a concrete example among many. Take for instance man's need for food. This is one of the most basic needs of the human body, because on its satisfaction depends human existence, and therefore one of the most demanding of all bodily needs. If you are hungry, there is literally a natural vacuum in your stomach demanding to be filled with food. Now, since nature abhors vacuum, it will not rest until you do something to fill up that vacuum. Otherwise, you will feel pain so nagging, excruciating, and demanding that you will be compelled to do things you normally will not do—like stealing, cheating, or even killing—only to fill up that vacuum to end your agony. And when you have finally taken food and finally filled that natural vacuum, what do you feel? Naturally, you will feel satisfied and experience great relief because you have filled the vacuum and have done what nature wanted you to do. So nature rewards you with the pleasurable feelings of satisfaction, fulfillment, and great relief. Now, that satisfaction and fulfillment of the need of your body for food which produced your pleasurable feelings of great relief and contentment, is not that happiness? Absolutely! That in simple graphic terms which can be understood by anybody is the simple dynamics of happiness with regard to man's basic need for food. Another example, which I know you will like best, is sex, which we will go into later.

Another aspect of happiness which we humans fail or refuse to see is that happiness seems elusive because it is always there with us. We humans have the mysterious tendency not to see something which is obvious. That is why the most difficult question to answer is the simple one because we fail to see the obvious simple answer while we search for the complicated one. That is why we have difficulty finding things that are staring at us while we are desperately looking for them in hidden places. That is why the best way to hide things, according to Sherlock Holmes, is to place them in open space because people will not think of looking for them there. This is the principle of hiding openly.

The same principle applies to happiness. Happiness is not hidden. That is why it is elusive. It is always within us. (As Jesus Christ said, "The kingdom of heaven is within you.") That is why we cannot find it because we are looking for it everywhere except where it can really be found: within us.

In sum, happiness is always with us because it is simply the fulfillment of human needs that ordinarily cannot be postponed. Now, what are these human needs and how should they be fulfilled? The answer to these fundamental questions brings us to our next chapter, "The Nature of Man," because these needs are basically grounded in man's integral nature. But before we go into that, there are two highly important issues that will shed more light to the subject and, therefore, should be addressed first. These issues are human pleasure and human wants vis-à-vis human happiness.

Happiness and pleasure are two different distinct entities. It is a grave mistake to mistake one for the other, a huge mistake many people easily commit for obvious reason. As we shall shortly see, this is the cause of a lot of human unhappiness. On one hand, happiness, as we have seen, is simply the fulfillment of human needs; pleasure, on the other hand, is the motivation and the reward humans get for fulfilling their natural human needs. Hence, happiness is an end, while pleasure is a means to that end. In our pursuit of happiness, we should always keep this essential distinction in mind; otherwise, we will easily be waylaid or lose our way and not reach our intended goal which is happiness. This is the tragedy of a lot of misguided people. They think pleasure is happiness and happiness is pleasure, and so all their life, they relentlessly pursue pleasure, only to find unhappiness waiting for them at the end.

Although pleasure is not happiness, it is the means to happiness. In that sense, pleasure is also an essential ingredient of human happiness. Let us elucidate this matter through a concrete simple example. Nature has a huge stake in the preservation of the human race which is composed of individual persons. To accomplish this, these individuals have to eat in order to survive so that the human species will also survive. Now, in order for these individual humans to eat, they have to have an incentive, a motivation, for them to eat. Indeed, they have. Nature took care of that. When they eat, nature gives them pleasure not only while eating but even after eating. And so, they eat. When people derive no pleasure in eating—like when they are sick—they refuse to eat because nature tells them not to eat by giving them no appetite so that the natural healing process will be enhanced. Hence, the pleasure people derive from eating is the means wise nature provides so that individual humans will live to maintain the human species. But as we said, we should not confuse eating per se from the pleasure we derive from eating. We eat in order to live and we derive pleasure in eating in order for us to eat. This principle should be crystal clear in our mind; otherwise, we will keep on eating for the mere pleasure of eating and not for the purpose of eating which is to satisfy our need for food. Then what happens is that instead of eating in order to live, we live in order to eat. Thus, a lot of people not only eat excessively but eat a lot of junk foods because they are delicious despite the negative impact to their health. When this happens, the natural purpose of eating is subverted and the fundamental law of nature is violated. And since we cannot violate the law of nature with impunity, we have to suffer the negative consequences of our negative acts. That is why we suffer from diseases resulting from overeating and eating the wrong kind of food. Then our goal of happiness disappears together with our precious life.

This brings us to another equally important issue: the distinction between food and nonfood. The failure to recognize this crucial distinction is another tragedy for a lot of misguided people. Deluded people think that everything that tastes good (delicious) is food. Well, they have to think again. Unfortunately, many of these so-called food, which are really delicious, are really nonfood because they are truly toxins that harm the human body. To avoid this tragedy, there is a crucial need to properly define "food," food for the human body, that is. For clarity and simplicity, let us define food as that which is fit for human consumption. The key word in this definition is "fit." This is a short word, but it speaks volumes and so it also needs to be defined. As I suspected, *Webster* has an almost voluminous definition of "fit." For our purpose, we will choose the simple word "suitable." Food, therefore, is that which is suitable for human consumption. And food is suitable for human consumption only if it fulfills the purpose for which it was created or made, namely, to maintain human life. Anything, therefore, which goes by the name of food but destroys instead of promoting or maintaining human life is not really food but nonfood or, if you will, junk food. An egregious example of nonfood but everybody erroneously thinks as food is the ubiquitous meat. This is a fact which escapes a lot of people, even those in the medical profession who are supposed to be knowledgeable on this issue. In my personal experience and that of others, eating meat is the cause of a lot of diseases, especially the major deadly diseases such as cancer and cardiovascular diseases of which up to now, Western medicine has no cure. And yet everybody eats meat. (Vegetarians are the extremely few exceptions.) Even medical doctors are either ignorant of this fact or simply ignoring it. The few ones I know advise their patients not to eat meat *only* when the latter are already sick of cancer or cardiovascular disease. (Surely, this does not speak well of the medical profession, to say the least!)

The importance to human health and happiness of not eating nonfood cannot be overly emphasized.

This subject has been extensively and sufficiently discussed in my previous book, *The Spiritual and Ethical Dimension of Vegetarianism*. That book defends the thesis that the only food suitable for human consumption is the vegetarian food which also has spiritual and ethical dimension.

Another extremely important issue which needs to be addressed regarding human happiness is the radical distinction between human needs and human wants. The proper understanding and realization of the existence and importance of this distinction is a cardinal requirement for the achievement of human happiness. If you do not know this distinction, then you will easily confuse the two and pursue the satisfaction of human wants instead of the fulfillment of human needs. If this happens, then you will never find happiness and your life will again be a total failure, a tragedy of immense proportion. Why? Simply because, as repeated ad nauseam, our natural and proper goal in life is to find happiness which is the fulfillment of human needs and not the satisfaction of human wants. Hence, we should define these terms for better understanding. For clarity and simplicity, let us define them in terms of human happiness as we have been doing all along. To repeat, human needs are those the fulfillment of which redounds to human happiness. Human wants, however, are those the fulfillment of which results in human pleasure. Human needs are definite and few. Human needs are those of the body, the mind, and the spirit. (We will discuss this in a later chapter.) Human wants however are indefinite, variable, and innumerable. Human needs can easily be fulfilled, whereas human wants can never be satisfied. Hence, the satisfaction of human wants is at best an elusive one. Therefore, a life spent in this pursuit is a total failure, to say the least.

However, the satisfaction of human wants is not altogether futile and useless, nor is it bad by any means. After you have fulfilled your human needs and therefore have achieved happiness, by all means, satisfy also your human wants in order to experience more pleasure to enhance your happiness. That is perfectly legitimate and much to be desired in order to achieve what Aristotle calls eudaemonia, the Greek word for "the good life." Hence, there is absolutely nothing wrong with enhancing your happiness with pleasure, provided it will not result in unhappiness. What is absolutely wrong is confusing happiness with pleasure so that you pursue pleasure, thinking it will give you happiness. That is a sure formula for a tragic life. The right approach is to pursue happiness first, and after you have succeeded in achieving happiness, then you can pursue pleasure. That will result in a successful life because you will be able to handle pleasure properly since you have already achieved happiness. A graphic illustration is our favorite example, eating. After you have taken your soup, salad, and the main course, your need for food is completely fulfilled and taken care of and you are, therefore, happy. If you still want to enhance your happiness, you may take some dessert as most people do. But do not confuse the dessert with the soup, salad, and main course so that you will only eat the dessert, as most children want to do because the latter gives them more pleasure. If you will do that regularly, then you will achieve not happiness but diabetes mellitus. This brings us to another important distinction between reasonable pleasure and unreasonable pleasure.

There are countless things in life which will give us pleasure. But this does not mean that we will avail of all of them for the simple common-sense reason that many of them will eventually destroy our health—and therefore our happiness—by merely using them (like drugs) or misusing them through excess (like alcohol). In this sense, not all pleasure is reasonable; some are indeed unreasonable. Consequently, we have to use our God-given power of discrimination and willpower in using them. Since there are countless numbers of things that will give us reasonable pleasure out there, it is the height of stupidity, if not insanity, to avail of things that will give us unreasonable pleasure. For our happiness, let us learn the important lesson that we cannot have everything in this life, that it is part of wisdom to be discriminatory and selective.

To recapitulate, a need is the lack or absence of a natural basic necessity which a living individual requires for survival. A need therefore demands to be fulfilled, like a vacuum, and the failure to do so causes suffering, but its fulfillment results in happiness. Happiness, therefore, is the fulfillment of the natural basic needs of a living individual. Pleasure, however, is the natural result or by- product of happiness and serves not only as a motivation to achieve happiness but enhances happiness as well. Want, however, is the desire to achieve pleasure, which can never be satisfied. Since some things that can give us pleasure can also give us unhappiness, it is part of wisdom to exercise discrimination in availing of things that can give us pleasure.

So there you are. Now you finally have the working knowledge to achieve happiness in this life and have a successful life. But knowledge is not enough. You have to have wisdom which is knowledge put into practice. Without wisdom, knowledge is useless. Therefore, in order to really profit from this book and get your money's worth, you have to be wise and put your knowledge into practice for your own benefit, well-being, and happiness.

Chapter

3

Human Nature and Happiness

Man is a trinity. Man is a triune being composed of body, mind, and spirit.[19] The three dimensional aspect of physical, mental, and spiritual is encapsulated in the *unum substantiale* (one substance) that is man. As an unum substantiale, man functions as an integral being. This means that all man's activities are the result of the combination of his physical, mental, and spiritual being working and functioning together as one —always. It also means that whatever happens to any of the three essential components of man's being also affects the other two— always. It is therefore impossible to dissect man's activities and classify them as either physical, mental, and spiritual since these three aspects of his being contribute together as one in the production of these activities—always. In concrete, this means that it is not the mind or the brain that thinks, but it is the entire person who thinks. It means that it is not the heart or the mind which loves, but it is the entire person who loves.

Man, therefore, is a living contradiction. Man is both one and many, a unity in diversity. Thus, man is truly a microcosm (a small universe), an unsolved puzzle, an eternal mystery, a philosophical Gordian knot waiting for an intellectual Hercules to unravel it. Any attempt, therefore, to find a solution to the perennial human problem concerning happiness should bear this in mind in order that the attempt should have a holistic and not a fragmented approach and effect; otherwise, the attempt will be at best a sorry exercise in futility, if not in monstrous disaster.

Now, since man's body, mind, and spirit are the essential components of human nature, it follows that they are all equally important and have equal value. The emphasis is on the word "equal." This means, to highlight the obvious, that man's body, mind, and spirit should be given equal importance. One should not make a mistake on this extremely significant matter. To repeat, one should not treat one as more or less important than the others. This is a very salient point which cannot be overemphasized because it is one of the biggest stumbling blocks of a lot of people in all the span of human history including the present. An egregious example of this tragedy is the case of religious people—and they are legion, to borrow a biblical phrase—who were so enamored of the so-called spiritual life that they behave as though they were disembodied spirits. They not only deny their physical being its proper needs, like food, but even hate their body which they label as the instrument of the devil and a source of sins. Thus, they torture their poor body. This horrible practice was so prevalent during the dark ages. Today, it still exists but only in a minimal degree—perhaps. Its present-day existence is even featured in the famous novel of Dan Brown, *The Da Vinci Code*, in the case of the murderous monk who tortured his body and considered it a virtuous act.

However, the prevalent irrational practice of so-called religious people nowadays concerning their body is simply to neglect it or abuse it. Their main object in life is to develop to the full their mind and spirit but neglecting in the process the proper care of their body, or worse, abuse it. When their body finally succumbs to diseases caused by their unhealthy lifestyle consisting of eating the wrong kind of food, overeating, smoking, drinking, and failure to exercise regularly, if at all, they suffer patiently like a martyr and take their suffering as a will of God, as though it was God who made them sick. Eventually, their suffering is ended, together with their aspiration to perfect their mind and soul, by death. Such is the tragic fate of those who live in violation of their nature as the triune being of body, mind, and spirit.

This brings us once again to the crucial significance of the dynamics of human happiness. Happiness is simply fulfilling the needs of your body, mind, and spirit, and since your body, mind, and spirit operate as one, in a holistic manner, so also your providing their needs should be done in a holistic manner. This means that one should always maintain a healthy balance among the three members of the supreme trinity component of one's life. In concrete, an athlete, for instance, despite his obsession in maintaining the athletic prowess of his body should also maintain the health of his mind and spirit by engaging in proper intellectual and spiritual activities so that he would be not only a well-balanced person but, more importantly, a happy one. Another concrete example is the case of Buddha. Before he achieved his Buddhahood, Buddha punished his body by doing excessive ascetic practices such as rigorous fasting, thinking that he would achieve enlightenment by doing so. When these abnormal practices failed, he was forced to fulfill his natural need. He ate. With the need of his body satisfied, he went on to satisfy the need of his mind and spirit by meditating under the bodhi tree. Tradition tells us that it was only then that he achieved enlightenment and became Buddha (the enlightened one). Thus, he preached about the "middle path," the path of moderation as a necessary means for achieving a happy life and spiritual perfection.20 Hence, one should always maintain balance in life by always avoiding anything in excess. It is a difficult task, to be sure, but it can be done and must be done if one wants to be happy and have success in life. And remember that "balance" means addressing the needs of man's body, mind, and spirit in a holistic manner and avoiding excess.

As I am writing this chapter, a most serious problem involving the whole world is unfolding before my eyes as I watched CNN's coverage of the horrible crisis in Syria. The specter of thousands of poor Syrians fleeing from the wrath of ISIS militants literally brought tears to my eyes. How can this unspeakable evil and insanity be happening to supposedly intelligent rational human beings? A cogent analysis of the situation will eventually reveal that, again, the ultimate problem lies in the failure of us humans to find happiness. If people cannot find happiness, they can and will always find war. That is the tragic truth of the human situation. That is the tragic truth of human nature. This tragic truth is now being played out in Syria, Iraq, Afghanistan, and elsewhere.

But this tragic situation need not happen. Humans can still be saved. There can still be peace on earth. All that is needed is a proper understanding and proper implementation of the simple dynamics of human nature regarding happiness.

This brings us to the next three chapters wherein a more thorough and comprehensive discussion of human nature and its relation to happiness will be made extensively.

Chapter

4

The Human Body

Health is wealth. Indeed, the health of your body is not only your wealth, but more importantly, your happiness as well. It is impossible for you to be happy if you are sick and suffering from excruciating pain. Therefore, you should always bear in mind that the primary need of your body is health. And if your body is deprived of that essential need and it becomes irrevocably sick, then your mind and your spirit also suffer and that is the end of not only your happiness but eventually your own very life as well. Hence, the supreme lesson you should learn in life is: no matter what you do, never compromise the health of your body; otherwise, everything you do will be an exercise in absolute futility.

The supreme primordial question, therefore, to be sufficiently answered is: how can you be always healthy? I have discussed this issue at length and addressed it thoroughly in my two previous books, but I do not mind doing it again. My formula for human health is simplicity itself. It is the same formula with regard to your car's health. If you want your car to be always in good condition, you should do five essential things for your car. They are the following:

1. You should give your car the right kind of fuel.
2. You should give your car enough exercise.
3. You should give your car enough rest.
4. You should always keep your car clean.
5. You should pay attention to your car's needs.

Your body, like your car is also a machine, a most sophisticated machine no doubt, but a machine nevertheless. Therefore, the same treatment you give your car to maintain it in tiptop condition also applies to your body—mutatis mutandis. Let us walk through these five essential services you give your car and see how they compare with the way you should take care of your body.

1. You give your car the right kind of fuel. If your car is running on gasoline, you do not give it kerosene or diesel. You give it ordinary gasoline, or if you have money to spare, you give it premium gasoline because these are the right and best fuel, respectively, for your car. Why is this so? Because the engine of your car was designed to feed on gas, that is why. If you will violate the design of your car and give it the wrong kind of fuel, you know exactly what will happen to your car. Now, with regard to the human body, what kind of food did nature design the human body to feed on? To answer this, we have to examine the human body's digestive, absorptive, and excretory systems whose functions are directly connected with the food the human body takes. The body's digestive system consists of the mouth and the stomach. The body's absorptive and excretory systems consist basically of the small and big intestines, respectively. The digestive, absorptive, and excretory systems of the human body were designed by nature to digest, ingest, absorb, and excrete only fruits, nuts, and vegetables. Thus, our front teeth (the incisors) are sharp, designed obviously by nature for biting fruits, nuts, and vegetables, which are then chewed by our blunt molars and premolars, designed obviously by nature for chewing.

Interestingly, carnivorous animals, like lions and tigers, who do not chew the meat they eat but simply swallow them, do not have molars and premolars. They only have sharp canines and incisors designed obviously by nature for killing and biting their prey.

Our stomach is not that strong. We easily get indigestion. Compared with the stomach of carnivorous animals, like the snake which can swallow one whole animal and digest it, our stomach is weak and designed obviously by nature to digest easily digestible foods like fruits, nuts, and vegetables.

Our intestines, which absorb and eliminate the food the stomach digested, are very long and obviously designed by nature to eliminate from the body easily digestible vegetarian food. If we eat animal flesh, which is hard to digest, it will stay too long and rot in our stomach and very long intestines, causing toxins that cause diseases in the human body. That is why people who eat meat develop cancer and all sorts of diseases.

The nature of man's digestive, absorptive, and excretory systems are incontrovertible proofs that man is designed by nature to eat products of the plant kingdom and not of the animal kingdom. If man will violate nature's design—as man is doing now by eating animal flesh—he will have to suffer the terrible consequences of his stupid action by incurring terrible diseases. No one violates nature with impunity.

1. You give your car enough exercise. You let your car run every day. Or at least you let the engine of your car run even for a short while every day. If you do this to your car because it is a machine and needs this kind of exercise, a fortiori, you should also give your body enough exercise every day for the same reason.

2. You give your car enough rest. If you don't and let it run for almost twenty-four hours every day, I am sure you know what

will happen to your car. Therefore, the more reason you should give your body enough rest.

3. You give your car a thorough cleansing regularly. You should also do likewise and with more reason to your body. You can find many good books on the subject of body cleansing and detoxification. I also wrote on this subject in my book, *The Universal Medicine*, which is now in circulation.

4. You pay attention to your car's needs. Your car communicates with you through its many gauges. So you have to pay attention to them closely and act accordingly. When your car says it needs gas or water or oil, you better give it to your car right away or else...so also with your body. You have a symbiotic relationship with your body. You cannot do anything without your body and vice versa. Indeed, you are so intimately related with your body that you even think you are your body. So love your body and listen to it. It communicates with you always through your feelings. When it needs food, you feel hungry. When it needs water, you feel thirsty. When it needs sex, you feel horny and so on. When your body tells you what it needs, you better listen to it and act accordingly. Our problem is we pay attention to our body more when it needs sex than when it needs food. That is why people get sick of gastric ulcer by not eating regularly and of venereal disease by overindulgence in sex. So if you want to be healthy, treat your body with respect. Listen to it and act accordingly.

There you are. With the five essential services enumerated above, you now have a complete basic knowledge of how to maintain your good health all your life and therefore avoid getting sick. Without this most important basic knowledge on the most important basic necessity of life which is health, all other knowledge is useless.

Apropos of this vital matter, let me share with you some nuggets of wisdom I gleaned from the internet's Shirley's Wellness Café: "According to the World Health Organization: 'Health is more than the absence of disease. Health is the state of optimal well-being.'

Optimal well-being is a concept of health that goes beyond the curing of illness to one of achieving wellness. Many of us have been brought up to believe that our health depends solely on the quality of the healthcare we receive. The truth is, your health is your responsibility. You are the only person who must make the steps to preserve your health and promote your wellness. Only you have the power to create wellness for yourself."

The above trove of wisdom speaks for itself. If you are wise, you will not only listen to it—and listen carefully and wisely—but more importantly, make it a wonderful reality in your life.

In sum, take good care of your body religiously so you will be happy and enjoy life. Do not make the terrible mistakes of people who pursue their dreams—whatever those are—but neglect the care of their body in the process. Poor people, when they have finally found their dreams, they can no longer enjoy them because they are about to die of diseases caused by neglecting their body. What a tragedy! Indeed, a tragedy which could have been easily avoided by simply loving and taking care of their body.

Health is more than wealth. It is happiness.

5

The Human Mind

If you are your body, you are also your mind, and with more reason, since your consciousness, the basis of your personality (your ego), is grounded in your mind. Hence, you should love and take good care of your mind as you love and take good care of yourself.

If the well-being of the human body is essential for human happiness, as repeatedly emphasized ad nauseam, so is the well-being of the human mind. Hence, if you want to be happy, you should also take good care of your mind religiously. How? First, you should take good care of your brain. Why? Because your brain is the physical organ of your mind or, if you will, the brain is the bodily instrument of your mind. (A violin virtuoso, no matter how brilliant, cannot produce music from a defective violin.) Since your brain is a part of your body, taking good care of your body necessarily includes taking good care of your brain and vice versa. Thus, the crucial significance of the previous chapter about man and his body and the momentous implication of the cardinal principle previously discussed that man is an unum substantiale (one substance): a trinity of body, mind, and spirit functioning in total seamless unity. Your brain, mind you, is not just a part of your body. It is the most important part of your body. It is nature herself who tells us of the supreme role of the brain by putting it on top of the body and protecting it with a thick human skull designed like a helmet for optimum protection. You should therefore follow nature's example by giving priority to your brain without neglecting the other parts of your body. You should always protect your brain by not engaging in dangerous sports, like boxing, that will eventually damage your brain. There are many sports out there that give benefit to your body as well as your mind because they not only exercise your body in general but also your brain in particular. You should not also take anything that will damage your brain. I am referring to drugs, which include cigarette and alcohol. These dangerous substances damage not only your brain but also the other vital organs of your body like your lungs, stomach, liver, and your heart. I know so many people who allowed themselves to be literally slaves of cigarettes and alcohol, and they end up dying of cancer of their vital organs. These stupid people include priests, doctors, lawyers, diplomats, engineers, and other professionals whom one expects to know better than allow themselves to be sorry slaves of vices. But unfortunately, their faulty education did not prepare them for a healthy life.

You should adopt the motto which I learned in college: "Mens sana in corpore sano" (A sound mind in a sound body). This is an ideal which you and everybody, for that matter, should espouse and pursue. It is an ideal which is not an illusion but something which can easily be realized and absolutely doable if you have the knowledge and the will to make it a beautiful reality in your life so that you can be happy and enjoy life to the full. This book will give you that knowledge. It is up to you to make it a wonderful reality in your wonderful life so that your life will be a complete success.

And so, to continue our topic, how should you take care of your brain so that you will have a healthy mind? Aside from protecting zealously your precious brain, you should nourish it properly by giving it its proper food, the brain food. Do you know the proper food for your brain? All the major organs of the body: the brain, the heart, the lungs, the liver, etc., have their proper food. It is part of wisdom, or at least common sense, to have this visceral knowledge at your fingertips. Unfortunately, common sense and especially wisdom are not that common. The educational system of the world, especially the Western world, is basically flawed because it does not teach this knowledge which is obviously essential and crucial to man's well-being. Consult my two previous books, *The Spiritual and Ethical Dimension of Vegetarianism* and *The Universal Medicine*, for a thorough discussion of this momentous subject.21

To continue, aside from proper nourishment, your brain also needs proper exercise. Is this something new to you? Yes, your brain is a muscle, and like the other muscles of your body, it needs exercise. If you will not provide your brain that vital need, then like any other muscle, it will also atrophy and you will be a hapless victim of the dreadful Alzheimer's disease. Not a pleasant prospect, isn't it? Hence, you should maintain your brain, like your whole body, in proper, optimum shape by giving it proper exercise. Again, do you know how to do that? If you don't, then here it is: *thinking*.

Yes, thinking. And what is thinking? *Webster* defines the word as follows: Thinking is the "action of using one's mind to produce thought."22 The significant words in this definition are: "using one's mind." Yes, to think is to use one's mind. The problem is, in this age of television, computer, and cellphones, it seems people no longer use their mind. They stare blankly at the screens of these machines the whole day. And nobody reads anymore, except of course, the text messages. No wonder the dreadful Alzheimer's disease is getting more prevalent and might soon develop into a pandemic—if people will continue the dreadful habit of not using their mind and, of course, their brain as well.

I remember the good old days when there was no television and computers, and cellphones were not even the stuff of dreams. People then, even old ones, have no problem remembering things. They died of old age with all their mental faculties intact. But nowadays, it is absolutely shocking to encounter people at their middle age, and even young ones, already with memory problems. What is happening to the human race? Is the law of evolution no longer working so that devolution is now the new norm? It is absolutely tragic that people do not realize this tragic fact. I am therefore making this wake-up call. It is time people should wake up and be made aware of what is happening negatively to their precious lives. It is time they should be made aware that not everything in this modern civilized world is positive and redounds to their welfare. And they can only do this if they think, if they use their own brain.

Fortunately, humans are designed by nature to think. This is clearly shown when young children question everything and keep on asking "why?" nonstop to the agony of their parents. But unfortunately, when children eventually grow up, they stop asking questions and join the bandwagon of nonthinking adults. And in this day of computers, they become victims of this modern-day monsters. Children no longer think because they are so enamored of the computer games they play every day and almost the whole day. This modern-day phenomenon negatively affects children's mental health as well as social behavior according to psychologists and sociologists. Instead of playing with other children and thereby hone their social behavior, they play with computers. In the process, they lose the benefits of human interaction with their peers, benefits that are essential in the proper development of their mind, character, and personality. Thank God, I was not born and did not grow up during this computer age. And I refuse to be its victim.

What about you? Will you allow yourself to be a sacrificial lamb to this modern-day idol? If you won't, then take control of your life. Be a master once more of your mind. Regain the lost glory that was once yours during your childhood days when you were a thinker, a philosopher. Question everything! Nothing should be sacred to the scrutiny of your mind, not even God. Question his supposed existence. Does God really exist? Why? What are the evidences for God's existence? Thomas Aquinas, one of the greatest Catholic Church's philosophers and theologians, posited five natural proofs (the "Quinque Viae") for the existence of God. However, Immanuel Kant, one of the greatest German philosophers, said that God's existence cannot be proven nor disproven. Who is right, Aquinas or Kant? Why? Or are they both wrong? Why? So think! For all you know, you might be more brilliant than both of them combined. But you can only know that if you think, if you use your mind. So think!

It is not really that difficult, you know. It is really the easiest thing in the world when you get accustomed to it. Just like exercising your other muscles, exercising your brain is a tad uncomfortable at the beginning. But as you progress, you will experience great pleasure not only because of the exhilarating sense of accomplishment but also because your brain produces pleasure giving natural opioids that give you the experience of euphoria, another word for the common term "high." Don't believe me. Try it yourself! Brain exercise or thinking is really addictive. And it is the best kind of addiction. Not only is it not prohibitive and dangerous, it is also free and useful. So avail of it.

Thinking involves asking yourself a lot of questions. Ask questions about anything and everything. Do not take anything for granted. As previously stated, nothing should be sacred to your inquiring mind. Inquire about the meaning and purpose of life, the truth about heaven and hell, the dogmas of religion, the relevance of sorrow and pain in human life, the problem of evil, the meaning of love, the problems of human life, etc., the list is endless. Make sure you know the answers to questions regarding these matters. Hence, you should not rely on the answers of anybody no matter how wise and knowledgeable he seems to be. The only authority you should recognize and rely on for any answer to any question is yourself, your own mind. Hence, you should not take anything by faith. Faith is the antithesis of truth. You will find that out when you start thinking. As Krishnamurti aptly puts it: "There is no path to reality any more than to truth. All authority of any kind, especially in the field of thought and understanding, is the most destructive evil thing. Leaders destroy the followers and the followers destroy the leaders. You have to be your own teacher and your own disciple. You have to question everything that man has accepted as valuable, as necessary."[23]

Thinking also involves a lot of reading. Thinking needs experience and knowledge as fodder for thought. With your limitations, you simply cannot experience and know everything there is to experience and to know. To fill these gaps, you should read a lot to encounter the experience and knowledge of other people who may be wiser and knowledgeable than you. By reading a lot, I mean *a lot*: read everything you can get hold of. Do not buy this hogwash called censorship that the Catholic Church espouses. Be your own censor. One of the objectives of reading is for you to exercise your critical thinking, which is a mental exercise. To be able to do this, you should read anything and everything including those materials that religion brands as "immoral." Nothing is immoral in this life. Immorality is only in the mind of those people who judge things as immoral. Hence, do not be choosy in your reading. But be choosy in accepting as your own the ideas that go through the mill of your critical thinking. Hence, in your reading, have an open and unprejudiced but critical mind regarding anything you read without exception including and especially those which ignorant people call holy books. These so-called holy books are the most dangerous of all reading materials. They are the causes of wars and other vicissitudes that plague the world even now. So read them with an open and critical mind and find out how these so-called holy books have influenced the so-called evil of this world. Find out how people, through their own fault and mistakes, have been misled by these so- called holy books, especially by the Bible in particular. The Bible, contrary to common misperception, is simply a historical book and, therefore, should be read accordingly. If read as a word of God, the Bible will definitely be a source of confusion and errors that are now wrecking havoc to human life.[24]

Thinking also involves making mistakes. Never be afraid to make mistakes. Everybody has a right to make mistakes. Making mistakes is an essential component of the dynamics of life and evolution. The path to knowledge and truth is not smooth and straight. It is bumpy and crooked. It is a path of trial and error and correction. But that is the beauty of it all. As the saying goes: "It is better to climb and fall than not to climb at all." Indeed, the path to success and glory is paved with a lot of mistakes.

Thinking also involves forming or developing proper attitudes or philosophy which will help you in your journey through life. You can do this by exploring and comparing different schools of thought regarding life and choosing what appeals to you at the moment.

Thinking also involves being able to change your attitudes or philosophy as you go along through life because life is a constantly changing process. This is what is called the "liberal" attitude as opposed to "conservative." "Liberal" comes from the Latin word "liber," which means "free." Freedom, therefore, should be the hallmark of your thinking, especially "freedom to change" in accord with the nature of ever-changing life. Hence, to be in tune with life, you should also change if change is being called for. Remember a free life is a happy life since the nature of man, who is endowed with free will, is essentially free. Remember what Patrick Henry famously said, "Give me liberty or give me death." Indeed, a conservative mind is a dead mind.

Thinking also involves thinking outside the box of public opinion. You should know by now that the majority of people whom we call the public or the hoi polloi are almost always wrong because they do not really think. They just follow. For them, thinking is a tedious, laborious process. Hence, they just follow. This is the bandwagon mentality, the mentality of nonthinking people that compose the public. Nietzsche calls them the herd for obvious reason. For me, it is much better to walk alone and be right than to ride in a wagon of people who are wrong.

Hence, thinking involves having the courage of your own conviction. Thinking is not for the many. It is only for the chosen few. So if you are a thinker, you will find yourself almost always alone because it is difficult to find another thinker. Hence, the place of a thinker is a lonely place. And it takes a lot of courage to stay there. However, despite being lonely, the place of a thinker is a glorious place.

Thinking involves being aware and knowledgeable about the problems of human life: what are the factors that produce these problems and what are the best way or means to solve them. For instance, one of the biggest problems of humans is the fact that there are already too many people in this small planet of ours. Every day, the number of people is increasing, but the area and resources of the planet remain the same. To add to the problem, mindless people who want to go on multiplying use the biblical injunction, "Go ye and multiply," to justify their prurient activities. Moreover, no one, not even any leader of the world, has come up with any solution to this problem, let alone talk about it. And worst of all, people behave as though there is no such problem. This reveals another serious human problem: that people in general do not really think. Hence, they are not aware that their failure to think results in many of their problems and sufferings which they attribute to God or to the devil, thus revealing their inability to really think correctly because they hardly think at all. Even highly educated people like those in the medical profession are guilty of this horrible fault. Their failure to think enables them to use their scientific knowledge to control death but not to control birth resulting in a natural imbalance causing the unnecessary proliferation of miserable old people adding to the endemic problem of population explosion.

Indeed, thinking involves a lot of things that you will discover when you start thinking. Therefore, do not get scared of thinking. It is the most natural thing for humans to do since humans are essentially rational animals, as the brilliant Greek thinker Aristotle said. And so, let your mind soar like an eagle in the heavenly realm of thought and experience the exhilarating joy that accompanies thinking. Let your mind explore the seemingly most difficult question which you are not able to answer at the moment. Be confident that sometime, somehow, the answer will pop up unbidden in your mind to your pleasant surprise, and like Archimedes, you will utter the famous word: "Eureka!" Then you will know that there is no question that cannot be answered. Then you will realize that the human mind is actually all-knowing—contrary to the erroneous perception of a lot of people—because the human mind is one with the universal mind.

Just as you allot a certain time to exercise your body, the more you should do the same to your mind. In my case, I enjoy doing it before sunrise, during sunset, and especially during a clear starry night. I wake up one hour before the sun peeps over the horizon and let my mind soar and play with the multicolored sky. And when the sun slowly and gingerly shows its brilliant face over the hills, I welcome it with gratitude for another newborn day full of abundant blessings and exciting promises. During sunset, when the sky is bathed with glorious splendor as the sun once again bids goodbye to the world he just showered with equal generosity and magnanimity to all, I let my mind join the sun in awe at this mystery of creation, and then willy-nilly, my mind expands in boundless unspeakable unity with the essence of life. A clear starry night, however, is pure mental and spiritual magic. As I gaze with pure abandon at the transparent sky blooming with myriad stars, I lose myself completely among the million galaxies of the universe, with my mind and entire being suffused with incredible wonder and awesome bliss.

During and after these incredibly wonderful moments, wonderful thoughts simply come unbidden to my receptive and fully energized mind. Thus, I do not even have to make an effort to think. My mind does its own thinking for me. That is the beauty and advantage of taking time to take care of the health of my mind. My grateful and generous mind rewards me with abundant priceless gifts. Your mind will do the same for you if you take care of it.

After giving your mind its own brand of gymnastics, the next proper thing to do is to give it its needed rest. Rest is always an integral part of activity. You cannot have a good fulfilling activity unless you have a good fulfilling rest. That is why a restful night is essential to a fruitful active day. Similarly, a satisfying mental rest is essential to a fruitful mental activity. That is a natural law which you can violate at your own peril. Actually, the mind, since it is a spiritual faculty, does not need rest. However, since it is intimately connected with the human brain which needs rest, the mind also shares the same need. Again, this is a manifestation of the reality that man is a triune being: a trinity of body, mind, and spirit.

Now, how do you give rest to your brain and therefore to your mind? The same way you give rest to your body: by sleeping. Sleeping does not necessarily mean the long night sleep of seven or eight hours. During the day, whenever you feel tired and drowsy after a physical or mental activity, that is the way nature is telling you to rest. So be wise and obey nature. It is best to take a catnap for few minutes. You will be surprised how that short rest can give you a lot of energy to spend for your next activity. Some misguided individuals fight and disobey nature by drinking coffee or tea, smoking, or taking other drugs to keep them awake. To be sure, these will keep you awake but the quality of your activity will suffer—even your health. You simply cannot violate nature with impunity. No one can!

Another natural way of getting another energy boost when you are tired is by doing meditation. By that, I do not mean the meditation practiced by the clergy which consists of thinking about so-called holy matters like the lives of the saints or the crucifixion of Jesus, etc. This kind of meditation will make you more tired because instead of resting your mind and your brain, they will still be working over these thoughts. The kind of meditation I am referring to is transcendental meditation which enables the mind to transcend its multitude of thoughts and go to a mental level where there is no thought and, therefore, a place of peace and quiet where the mind can get its needed rest even for a few seconds or minutes. Spiritual pundits call this region of the mind the "absolute" because it is devoid of any relative activity and things such as thinking and thoughts. As such, the absolute realm is a spiritual one where the mind, being spiritual by nature, truly finds its spiritual home. Thus, this type of meditation is essentially a spiritual exercise which is practiced regularly in the morning and in the evening for half an hour by spiritual individuals. Scuba divers like me call this mental diving. The surface of the sea is usually rough and filled with waves. To escape this stressful situation, scuba divers simply dive into the bottom of the sea where serenity and quiet reign supreme. There they find peace. So also, the surface of the human mind is rough and filled with stressful thoughts. To escape this stressful situation, one has to dive into the absolute realm of the mind where there is no thought. There, the mind finds rest and peace. This is the type of meditation which Jesus was practicing. The Bible says that after a stressful day of preaching, Jesus goes to the Garden of Olives and prays to his heavenly Father. If you want peace, simply meditate and find peace within you. This is the meaning of Jesus's words: "The kingdom of heaven is within you."

There is another dimension of the human mind which is normally hidden from people in general because it can be used either for good or evil and therefore is dangerous if used by the wrong person. I am referring to the all-powerful character of the human mind that the human mind is the genie in Aladdin's magic lamp. Because of its awesome power, the human mind is disguised as a genie or a fairy godmother in folktales all over the world.

The human mind is a creator. As such, it partakes of and shares with the creative power of the divine Creator. Everything created by man is created by the awesome power of the human mind. Think about it. The tallest and biggest building in the world, the biggest ship that ever sailed the mighty ocean, the biggest and fastest plane that ever crossed the boundless sky, the most powerful weapon ever invented, nay, everything momentous, humongous, and even seemingly insignificant things that originated from man's labor came from the creative power of the human mind. In sum, the entire modern world is a mental creation.

Ayn Rand, of all modern philosophers, has a remarkable realization and meaningful appreciation of this staggering power of the human mind. In one of her monumental opera, she impressively captured this awesome aspect of human nature by writing to the effect that a genuine house of worship should be such that when a human being enters it, that person should feel that he or she is not the subject but the object of worship. Wow! This idea is truly revolutionary, to say the least. To her everlasting credit, Ayn Rand, with one stroke of her powerful pen, has totally demolished the orthodox religious teaching, which is at best dubious, that man should worship God who, by the way, does not need nor demand to be worshipped. Ayn Rand, again to her everlasting credit, has a vision keen enough to penetrate the elusive veil of religious phantasy and expose its misleading phantom in order to reveal the truly awesome nature of man as divine.

No wonder, humans love to create and spend their whole life creating. In this wonderful process, they are able to exercise and exhibit their divinity, an activity truly exhilarating and fulfilling because it enables them to be in touch with their real divine self. By creating, humans cease to be mere humans and are transformed into gods. That is the thesis of Ayn Rand. That is also the thesis of this book.

This may sound blasphemous, as it also sounded blasphemous when Jesus categorically and fearlessly proclaimed to the high priest of the Jewish religion that he, the human Jesus, is God. Indeed, such is the power of the human mind that it can transcend crucifixion and death on the cross.

However, there is another dimension to the human mind—and it is a dark one. All the so-called evils of this world is also created by the human mind. The human mind is the devil in disguise. That is why I mentioned earlier that the human mind is dangerous. To be sure, it is a powerful instrument for good. However, it is also a powerful instrument for evil by misguided souls. It is a double- edge sword which cuts both ways. It should therefore be handled and wielded properly; otherwise, it can and will wreck havoc to human lives. This brings us to the most important aspect of the human mind.

Your mind is both your best friend and your worst enemy. It can bring you to the heavenly realm of your godhood. It can also dump you to the hellish point of human misery. If you can master your mind, it becomes your most valuable friend. But if you allow it to master yourself, then you become an unfortunate victim to your worst enemy. Whichever way the cookie crumbles, as the expression goes, the result entirely depends on you.

But remember the poet's admonition: "I am the master of my fate, I am the captain of my soul."

Chapter

6

The Human Spirit

Man is God in disguise. Or as the renowned Jesuit philosopher and paleontologist Pierre Teilhard de Chardin aptly said, "Man is not a human being having divine experience but a divine being having human experience." This is the inevitable conclusion that logically follows from our discussion at the last part of the previous chapter. If only humans will realize this sublime truth and act on it accordingly by behaving not as sinful humans, as erroneously taught by religion, but as real children of God and therefore divine, then assuredly there will be peace on earth. This esoteric truth is the magic key which everybody is looking for to open the magical door to happiness and peace in this life. This key was already revealed by Jesus Christ, as previously mentioned, but the Jews, instead of accepting it with gratitude, brutally repudiated it by crucifying him. Hence, happiness and peace on earth is still a beautiful dream.

That is the supreme human tragedy. Can you imagine if there is truly peace on earth? We unfortunate humans, instead of spending our precious time, limited resources, and wasting our psychic and physical energy by engaging in the purely insane and senseless acts of fighting and killing one another, should unite and collaborate to discover all the wonderful laws of nature that would enable us not only to erase poverty, hunger, and diseases all over the world, but also to prevent all the natural disasters such as earthquakes, typhoons, tornados, etc. that make life on earth more miserable. Having accomplished all these wonderful miracles, humans would then be able to invent all the amazing machines that would take us safely, conveniently, and speedily all over the terrestrial and marine world as well as throughout the universe. Then, we humans would be able to realize all our dreams in consonance with the principle that whatever the mind conceives, the mind achieves.

But sadly, all of the above still remain as humanity's fabulous dreams—all because up to now, we humans still refuse to accept that crucial key. The irony of it all is that Christians, who proclaim themselves followers of Christ, also repudiate vehemently this essential key to human salvation for which Christ gave his very life. This is the reason why humans cannot find happiness. This is the reason why there is no peace on earth.

But why should the realization that man is not just man but in fact divine, that man is a spark of the divine fire, a drop of the infinite ocean, why should man's knowledge of this wondrous truth bring peace and happiness to the beleaguered, wounded world? Christ gave the all-important answer to this all-important question when he said, "Know the truth and the truth shall set you free."

Man has long been imprisoned behind the bars of ignorance of his real nature—a fact which is promoted by the priests, rabbis, imams, ministers, and other leaders of religions whom Christ appropriately called as "the blind leading the blind." This tragic state of affairs naturally prevents humans from behaving and living properly as the perfect children of God: happy, righteous, and peaceful. The result? Humans became addicted to violence. Hence, there is a culture of violence all over the world. Thus, the gruesome specter of man's inhumanity to man—even in the name of God—became the human norm.

"Know the truth and the truth shall set you free" is the urgent message of the voice of Christ knocking at the door of every man's heart. But the door refuses to open.

However, why is knowledge of the truth necessary so that the truth shall set one free? Cannot the truth per se without knowing it set one free? The answer lies in the fact that unless one has knowledge of a thing, that thing is useless for him because as far as he is concerned, it does not exist. If a man for instance has a million dollars in the bank but he does not know it, for him, that million dollars is nothing because as far as he is concerned, it does not exist. The same is true with truth. There is no scarcity of truth. Truth is everywhere. But unless we know it, for us, it does not exist. Hence, useless. And we remain imprisoned in ignorance. That is why Christ said, "Know the truth and the truth shall set you free." But it is not enough to simply know the truth so that the truth shall set us free. It is implied that after knowing the truth, we should act accordingly in consonance and conformity with the truth.

It is clear, therefore, that man should know the sublime truth that he is literally, not just figuratively, the child of God, that he is divine and not the sinful creature that religion made him to believe so that he will be free to act and behave in a divine manner. This is in accordance with the metaphysical principle that action follows being, which means that one acts in accordance with his nature, which means that in order to "do" good, one must first "be" good, not the other way around, the way religion teaches. Christ's teachings are replete with this cardinal principle: "Even so, every good tree bears good fruit, but a bad tree bears bad fruit. A good tree cannot bear bad fruit, nor a bad tree bear good fruit" (Matthew 7:17–18; Luke 6:43–44). "A good man out of the abundance of his heart brings forth good; and an evil man out of the evil treasure of his heart brings forth evil" (Luke 6:45; Matthew 12:35). Surely, Christ could not have said it any better and clearer. Surely, the teacher par excellence could not have translated this abstruse metaphysical principle that "being" is the cause and "doing" is its effect in a language so crystal clear that it can be understood by all—easily— except by the Catholic clergy that keeps on preaching the opposite dogma: "Do good, do good so that you will be good and go to heaven." This is the erroneous message priests keep on preaching in their pulpits all over the world ad nauseam, a message diametrically opposite to that of Christ's.

Christ has given man this simple formula for happiness and peace circa two thousand years ago. Two thousand years have flown by, but happiness and peace on earth is still but a dream. Is there a chance that this dream will come true? Is Christ's mission a total failure? Despite all the signs to the contrary, despite all the discouraging events in the history of mankind, hope still springs eternal in the hearts of weary humans. It still does in the author's heart as shown by this book.

To continue, what does all of the above have to do with man and his spirit, the title of this chapter? It is simply this: man is essentially a spirit. This spirit is what we have been referring to as the divine, the spark of the divine fire, the drop of the infinite ocean. In other words, man is the Word made flesh, just as Jesus Christ is according to the Gospel of St. John: "In the beginning was the Word, and the Word was with God, and the Word was God...And the Word became flesh and dwelt among us" (John 1:1–14). If man is a son of God and humans are all children of God literally, as Jesus Christ said (John 10:34; Psalm 82:6), then why should we children of God inflict harm on one another? Why should we children of God not behave accordingly and really love one another so that there will be happiness and peace on earth?

The only answer is the fact that we humans still do not know our divine nature because we have not yet experienced and therefore do not know our godhood. Hence, Christ's words: "Know the truth and the truth shall set you free," really applies to us. The crucial question therefore is: how do we experience our spirit so that we will know that we are really children of God so that we will be free to act accordingly and behave in harmony with our divine nature? Since our spirit is immaterial in nature, it cannot be experienced by our senses that are designed by nature to experience only sensible or material objects. Fortunately, we humans are equipped with a faculty which has the same immaterial nature as our spirit. That immaterial faculty is our mind or consciousness. With our mind, we can then experience our spirit. How? The technique is called transcendental meditation as explained in the previous chapter. Through the process of transcendental meditation, the mind is able to transcend itself and go beyond its thoughts and reach the spiritual dimension where our spirit resides. It is a dimension which the pundits call the absolute since it is devoid of anything, even of the ubiquitous human thoughts. In that spiritual absolute dimension, the mind is in a state of unbounded awareness since the spiritual world is boundless. It is then that the mind experiences spiritual fulfillment and thus also experience absolute peace.

Therefore, transcendental meditation is the process by which we are able to experience our spirit, our real self, the kingdom of God within us, and thus, we are able to know without any shadow of doubt that we are really divine and therefore will behave accordingly as children of God, full of love for one another and for all creatures of God who are also God's children. This truth is of such paramount importance in our life that it is the key to our happiness and eventually to peace on earth. Therefore, it is time for humans to learn transcendental meditation. It is time for man to know the truth of his divine nature so that he shall be free to charter a life of happiness and peace so that at long last, love, prosperity, happiness, and peace shall dawn upon mankind.

To underscore the supreme importance of transcendental meditation in Christ's mission to save mankind not from hell but from our hellish life, the Bible has provided another significant clue for us to discover this immense treasure. Remember the Gospel's account of the incident when the Pharisee Nicodemus came to visit Jesus by night? Jesus said to him, "'Most assuredly, I say to you, unless one is born again, he cannot enter the kingdom of God.' Nicodemus said to Him, 'How can a man be born when he is old? Can he enter a second time into his mother's womb and be born?' Jesus answered, 'Most assuredly, I say to you, unless one is born of the water and the Spirit, he cannot enter the kingdom of God'" (John 3:1–5). This is typical of Jesus. He loves teaching in riddles that confound people's minds—as it did to Nicodemus in this particular case. But poor Nicodemus is right. How can a person be born again a second time from his mother's womb? But poor Nicodemus is also wrong for taking Jesus's words literally. And so Jesus answered him: "Unless one is born of water and Spirit, he cannot enter the kingdom of God"—an answer which spawns more questions such as: how can one "die" so that one can be "born" again?

To be honest, like Nicodemus, this riddle of Jesus stumped me. I could not find any satisfactory answer to it until I experienced transcendental meditation. Let me explain. Before doing any religious or spiritual exercise, one usually makes use of water for ablution. This is especially true in the Middle East during the time of Jesus when people either walk barefooted or with sandals. Thus, before they enter the temple or synagogue to worship, they purify themselves by washing their dusty feet. The Muslims also do this even now. They wash their feet before they enter the mosque or their room to pray. The Catholics make a symbolic ablution by making the sign of the cross with holy water before they enter the church. In my case, I also perform ablution by washing my hands and face before I do meditation. This freshens me up for meditation. During meditation, after I sat comfortably, closed my eyes, relaxed my whole body and my mind by not concentrating on anything, after a while, my mind, after some time of playing with its thoughts which I simply watched, suddenly transcended itself by going into a thoughtless state of pure awareness. At this stage, I lost consciousness of everything, even my own body. I was aware of only one thing: that I was aware. Since I was dissociated from my own body and even from my own mind because I have no more thoughts but only pure awareness, I was then in union with my spirit, with my real self, the kingdom of God within me. If death is the dissociation of the body, mind, and spirit, then at this stage of my meditation, I was actually experiencing "death": I died. However, this spiritual state lasts only for few seconds or minutes, depending on the purity of my nervous system. So eventually, my consciousness became normal and I became aware again of my thoughts and my body. Thus, after having experienced momentary spiritual "death" by being aware only of my spirit, I was born again. This experience of dying and being born again happened several times during meditation. Hence, after having gone through this experience of being born again of water (ablution) and spirit (the spiritual exercise of transcendental meditation), then I realized that this is the meaning of Christ's words: "Unless one is born again of water and spirit he cannot enter the kingdom of God." In other words, Christ's seemingly mysterious words simply mean that you can access the kingdom of God within you by doing transcendental meditation by which your consciousness is freed from its usual awareness of your body and mind with its endless thoughts—usually stressful—and, for a change, experience peace by uniting with your spirit which is the kingdom of God within you as Jesus Christ said. In the process you "die" to your physical self—like when you actually die, your consciousness separates from your body—and then when your consciousness goes back to the normal state of being aware of your body, then you are "reborn" or born again. This, I suggest, is the real meaning of being "born again," which Christ told Nicodemus but eluded the poor guy together with the whole population of Christendom because they do not practice transcendental meditation.

In sum, transcendental meditation is a spiritual technique of experiencing the kingdom of God within you, your spirit, which Jesus Christ kept on talking about in the Gospel. In the process, you also experience "dying" and "being born again." And this is the only way to die while remaining alive and being born again without going back to your mother's womb. Is that not absolutely cool?

Moreover, transcendental meditation is not just a process of experiencing the kingdom of God within you and being born again. It is also the wonderful process which culminates in the attainment of perfect unity of the three components of your being: your body, mind, and spirit. During this process, your body remains perfectly still which enables your mind to transcend itself by going beyond its normal thoughtful state, which enables your consciousness to unite with your spirit, the kingdom of God within you. Also, this wonderful process results in your body experiencing complete rest and the stimulation of your endocrine glands, corresponding to your psychic centers called chakras in Hindu, resulting in your brain producing opioids called endorphins which make you experience ecstatic bliss. This was the so-called mystical experience of mystics like the Spanish monks Juan de la Cruz and Teresa de Avila who experienced soaring into ecstasy during their meditation because their nervous system was pure as a result of living simple non-stressful lives in the monastery and eating simple vegetarian food consisting of plain bread and plain vegetables without condiments as their way of exercising self-abnegation. Thus, their endocrine glands were easily stimulated when they prayed, resulting in their experiencing heavenly blissful ecstasy which, in their ignorance, they called mystical experiences. But it is no more mystical than the experience of a high when you take cocaine or opium.

The beneficial result of this blissful experience is considerable in terms of one's personal life. It is such an incomparable satisfying experience that other pleasurable experiences you can have pales in comparison to the intensity and absolute satisfaction of your entire being with this holistic blissful experience. It is holistic because, as I said, it involves your whole being: your body, mind, and spirit working in tandem. Thus, this experience gives you complete fulfillment which cannot be given by any other source of pleasure in the world, including drugs. Thus, you are completely weaned from your uncomfortable and problematic attachments to worldly pleasures because you have experienced and can always experience in meditation the ultimate pleasure: spiritual bliss. And if you are a drug addict, this experience of exquisite bliss will cure you of your addiction. Also, if you are addicted to sex, like those pitiful pedophile priests, your addiction will be cured by this heavenly experience. This is another reason why Christ called the spirit the kingdom of God within you because when you enter this kingdom, you experience not only happiness but absolute divine heavenly bliss. With this doctrine, Christ, in effect, was preaching that humans can achieve heavenly bliss even in this life—in contravention with the Catholic doctrine that heavenly bliss is found only in heaven after you experience physical death.

Another salutary effect of "entering" this kingdom of God within you is that since you are weaned from your attachment to worldly pleasures, then you can enjoy them better because this time, you are no longer under their spell and control. From the debilitating slavery to worldly pleasures, you have attained the exhilarating mastership over them. This is the world of difference between the man of the world and the man of the spirit: the former cannot really enjoy the world because he is a miserable slave to it; whereas, the latter can do what he pleases with the world because he is its master. This is the esoteric meaning of Christ's words: "Be in the world but not of the world." This is the real meaning of being master of one's self, like Jesus Christ. This is the real purpose of Christ's life: to teach us to be masters of ourselves and thereby experience absolute happiness and thereby redeem us from our slavery to ourselves and to the world. This is the real meaning of redemption, not Christ's dying on the cross.

Going back to our main theme, what is the relevance of happiness to the fact that man is a spirit? Since happiness for man is the fulfillment of his needs, as a spirit, man needs to experience his spiritual being so that he will know that he is really a spirit; otherwise, his being a spirit will have no reality for him at all, and thus, he cannot enjoy his being a spirit. This is similar to the case of a millionaire who does not know that he is that rich, as previously mentioned. Since that is so, that millionaire is really poor. And if he thinks he has a need to be rich, then he will be unhappy all his life until his need to be a millionaire is fulfilled. So also, man has to experience and thus know that he is a spirit; otherwise, a natural vacuum will be created within him, a vacuum which will demand to be filled by all means. And if he does not know how to do it, then he will be unhappy all his life. Since the need is a spiritual need, it can only be satisfied by a spiritual experience, the experience of knowing one's godhood. No other experience will do, much less the experience of acquiring material things in order to fill up the spiritual vacuum in one's self. That is the meaning of St. Augustine's words: "Lord, thou hast made us for Thyself and our heart cannot rest until it rests in Thee." This is the tragedy of a lot of people who, out of ignorance, spend all their life trying to acquire everything except the thing that really matters: the spiritual experience of knowing one's godhood. Then, at the end of the day, they realize that they have not found what they are looking for, that their quest for happiness was in vain, that their life is a total failure. Then eventually, they commit suicide. What a tragedy! And this is the tragedy that happens to many Hollywood celebrities.

But this tragedy can easily be avoided by practicing religiously the spiritual exercise of transcendental meditation together with living a normal life. This is the meaning of living a holistic life: a life of both matter and spirit. A serious seeker of spiritual life need not go to the Himalayas or enter a monastery in order to live a spiritual life and be happy. He simply has to practice transcendental meditation regularly while living a regular normal life so that he can acquire cosmic consciousness, a superior state of consciousness which is explained in the next chapter.

What other momentous lessons can we derive from all these narratives? One lesson, as previously mentioned, is that heaven is here and now and it is inside us. While we are alive and living in this world, the only heaven we can be sure of is the heaven within us, the kingdom of God within us—as pointed out by Jesus Christ himself.

And yet, we really do not know this kingdom of God within us. We do not know this wonderful world within us, the spiritual world. We are so familiar with our external world but so ignorant of our internal world. We are so enamored of the transient relative world, but we are not even concerned of the permanent absolute world. We are doing everything in our power to explore the outer space which has no bearing to our happiness, but we do not do anything even to have a glimpse of the inner absolute space within us which is essential to our happiness and well-being.

No wonder there is such a huge spiritual vacuum within us demanding to be filled. And since nature abhors vacuum, nature will always do everything in its power to fill up this spiritual vacuum. And since we are not doing anything to satisfy nature, the result is a never-ending war within us. No wonder we are so unhappy.

And yet the problem is so easy to solve. The only thing we have to do—which is very easy to do, easier than eating or having sex—is to have a change of consciousness through the practice of transcendental meditation. This brings us to another significant topic: consciousness, which is the subject of the next chapter.

Chapter

7

Consciousness and Happiness

We experience happiness through our consciousness. Thus, happiness and consciousness are intimately related. Moreover, the degree or level of our happiness depends on the degree or level of our consciousness. Thus, if we want to experience greater happiness, we should cultivate our consciousness so that we can achieve superior degree of consciousness. Unknown to many, we have seven different levels of consciousness: (1) sleeping, (2) dreaming, (3) waking, (4) transcendental, (5) cosmic, (6) God, and (7) unity consciousness.[25] Our experience of reality also depends on which level of consciousness we are in. People in general are familiar only with the first three levels of consciousness which we share with the animals. Hence, if our consciousness is limited only to sleeping, dreaming, and waking, we are no better than the animals in terms of consciousness. Perhaps, this is the reason why most people behave no better or even worse than the animals. But since we are more than animals—indeed, a superior kind—we can experience other kinds of consciousness, the ones enumerated above from 4 to 7. Transcendental consciousness is the one we experience when we do transcendental meditation. It is called transcendental consciousness because when we do transcendental meditation, as previously explained, our mind is able to transcend or go beyond its thoughtful state and experience a thoughtless state: the state of the absolute where there is "nothing" (no relative objects), not even thoughts. That is why it is called "absolute" in contradistinction with the "relative." Philosophy and religion call God the absolute because God is "pure being" in contrast with the "complex beings" of the relative world. God, therefore, is the absolute pure being, the "nothing" from whom "everything" (the relative world) comes. This is what is called creation which theology erroneously defines as the process of producing something out of nothing. Hence, make no mistake. The "nothing" that is God the absolute is not the "absence" of anything but the presence of infinite potency from which all relative reality (every "thing") comes. In this sense, therefore, God the absolute is both nothing and everything, the supreme contradiction. As nothing, God is the infinite potentiality from which all actuality comes. As everything, God is the infinite actuality of the infinite potentiality. If you do not understand this, neither do I. This only proves that God is still beyond our human understanding because we have not yet attained the proper consciousness for the proper understanding of God. That is why our main goal in life should be to continually increase the level of our consciousness until we attain the highest level which is unity consciousness.

To continue, therefore, transcendental meditation enables us to experience transcendental consciousness which is an experience of the absolute part of our being: our godhood, the spirit. Since we experience the relative world when we are in our waking state of consciousness and the absolute world in our transcendental state of consciousness, we, therefore, have a split or fragmented consciousness: one for the relative and another for the absolute. That explains our split or fragmented personality, which explains our split or fragmented behavior, which explains our multitude problems in life. What to do? We should develop a holistic consciousness which embraces at the same time both the relative and the absolute world. Can this be done? Absolutely! This brings us to cosmic consciousness: the consciousness of the entire cosmos, consisting of the relative and the absolute, at the same time and all the time. To develop cosmic consciousness, you should not only practice transcendental meditation regularly morning and evening so that your nervous system gets accustomed to the experience of transcendental consciousness, but also purify your nervous system by always eating sattvic food (the vegan food), doing yoga physical exercises regularly, and very importantly, living a life of minimum stress. Having done all these religiously, a time will come when you will be experiencing transcendental consciousness although you are not doing transcendental meditation. Or to put it another way, you will be experiencing the absolute world together with the relative world at the same time and all the time. This is cosmic consciousness: the consciousness of both the relative and the absolute world at the same time and all the time. This is as far as I can tell you about cosmic consciousness because I have not really and fully achieved it. I have only fleeting glimpses of it here and there, now and then, but that is all. Those fleeting glimpses, however, are mind-boggling, to say the least.

To continue, the next stage to man's perfection is God consciousness. If cosmic consciousness is mind-boggling, God consciousness is absolutely earth-shaking. By a stroke of serendipity, I have had the opportunity of experiencing God consciousness, but only for some few unforgettable hours. To give you a rough idea of my super-wonderful experience, imagine experiencing absolute bliss (similar but not quite to the pleasure of an extended orgasm). I felt such a pure unadulterated blissful pleasure coming out from my heart like the water coming out from a huge mountain spring that I could not help but keep on laughing until my heart could no longer take the overwhelming experience so much so that I felt I could literally die laughing. And so, I forced myself to somewhat lessen the intensity of the blissful feeling so my heart would not suffer. Then it dawned on me that this could be the similar experience of those people in the mental asylum who kept on laughing for no external reason at all. It also dawned on me that, perhaps, this is the truth of what Jesus Christ said, "The kingdom of God is within you."

Then a little later, I had the fantastic experience of seeing everything as new as though it was the first time I saw them. And not only new but so beautiful beyond description that everything

I saw, even a rusty bottle cap, literally grabbed my attention and admiration, leaving me in a state of delirious awe. I realized then that there is really nothing ugly, but everything is fantastically beautiful in this world. Perhaps, this is similar to what William Wordsworth experienced when he wrote these immortal lines: "There was a time when meadow, grove, and stream/The earth and every common sight/ To me did seem/Appareled in celestial light/The glory and freshness of a dream."[26] Or perhaps, this was also the same experience of the mystic poet William Blake when he wrote: "To see a World in a grain of sand/And a Heaven in a wild flower/Hold Infinity in the palm of your hand/And Eternity in an hour."[27]

Indeed, I was also then in eternity but for several hours—I lost count of the exact time. This narrative is just a mere shadow of the splendor of my experience of God's consciousness. It was really an incredible and unforgettable experience of heaven on earth. When my fantastic experience was slowly fading, I tried to hold it back but to no avail. And when it finally faded, I felt like, perhaps, the same way Adam felt when he was driven out of paradise. And I cried. Helplessly. Hopelessly.

The impact to my being of that awesome experience lasted for several eventful days. Then suddenly, it was gone. However, its priceless memory never left me nor will it ever leave me. And they will be my incontrovertible proof that indeed heaven is here and now, not in some unknown place up there which religion wants us to believe. We only have to develop the vision and ability to see and experience it. And it is only through the constant experience of transcendental consciousness that this can happen.

That was my fleeting experience of God consciousness, an experience so wonderful and overwhelmingly blissful that no other experience of mine can compare with it even slightly. That experience became my lifelong incentive to continue religiously my daily spiritual activity so that before I go on to another dimension of life, I will first be rewarded with the same or even better experience which is the experience of unity consciousness.

According to spiritual pundits, unity consciousness is God's consciousness and much, much more. It is the ultimate experience, accordingly. In this final stage of consciousness, one experiences—I imagine—the awesome unspeakable oneness of the totality of reality. This is truly difficult to imagine, let alone comprehend since we are so used to the multiplicity of things in this relative world we live in. We can only speculate that this is nothing less than the transcendental experience of our oneness with the absolute and the relative combined—whatever that is. Hence, it is an exercise of pure futility to imagine and to attempt to communicate this experience. As Zen Buddhism aptly says, "He who speaks does not know; he who knows does not speak."[28] And so, that is all I can tell you about unity consciousness.

Perhaps unity consciousness is the same experience Thomas Aquinas, that legendary Dominican monk, had when, reportedly after celebrating mass sometime in December 1273, he had a mystical experience so profound and overwhelming that he refused to write anything after that and then died six months later. On his deathbed, he wanted to burn all his books. Obviously, his mystical experience made him realize that all his so-called great books, the *Summa Theologiae* and *Summa Contra Gentiles*, were all meaningless. And yet in these books, he tells us that true happiness consists in a beatific vision of God, which can happen only when one dies and go to heaven where one can see God face-to-face. Obviously, Aquinas's profound mystical experience proved himself wrong, and he never recovered from the staggering traumatic shock of his overwhelming mystical experience of the divinity.

There is a huge lesson to be learned from Aquinas case: sudden experience of these overwhelming states of consciousness is truly dangerous. It is similar to taking an overdose of hallucinogenic drug like LSD. It can kill you, as it has done to those who, after taking carelessly an overdose of it, committed suicide or had a heart attack. Like drugs, mystical experience packs a lot of energy, and if your nervous system is not ready for it, it will surely be your own undoing, as it did to poor Thomas Aquinas. Hence, mystical experience should be taken in small doses over a period to allow your nervous system to get used to it so that when the big dose comes, like God consciousness or unity consciousness, your nervous system will be able to take it safely and will just leave you in speechless euphoria but not totally overwhelmed. This highlights the tremendous significance of doing religiously, day by day, the exercise of transcendental meditation daily, morning and evening, over a period. This way you are able to receive small doses of mystical experiences gradually. Unfortunately for Aquinas, with all his vaunted learning and brilliance, he had no knowledge of transcendental meditation, let alone the seven states of consciousness you just learned. Hence, you are more blessed than Aquinas.

In sum, human perfection is the evolution of human consciousness to divine consciousness. And since divine consciousness is infinite, human perfection is also infinite. Hence, there is no limit to human perfection just as there is no limit to divine perfection. This simply shows the veracity of Christ's message that man is divine, that God is man's heavenly Father.

The seven states of human consciousness mentioned here are by no means the only parameters of consciousness available to man. To paraphrase Shakespeare: there are more in heaven and earth than are dreamt of in human philosophy.[29] Indeed, the horizon of human perfection is infinitely beyond man's vision and imagination. That is the beguiling beauty of life and existence. Nevertheless, if you want to achieve supreme happiness in this life, you should aim for the supreme consciousness.

This is the ultimate challenge of life: to achieve the impossible dream.

Chapter

8

Knowledge and Happiness

Knowledge is the food of the mind. Hence, the mind is constantly hungry for knowledge. It is tireless in its pursuit of knowledge. It's thirst to have even a drop of the unknown is unquenchable. Happiness for the mind, therefore, is the satisfaction of its need for knowledge. Again, if this essential need of the mind is not satisfied, a vacuum in man's being will be created. And since nature abhors vacuum, a person who has this problem and does not know this particular dynamics of human nature will be forced willy-nilly by his own nature to look for substitute to fill the vacuum. But since only knowledge can fill the need of the mind, no substitute will be good enough. This is the problem that causes a lot of unhappiness for a lot of people who are ignorant of this fact. This is the reason why people turn to alcohol, drugs, and other vices in their desperate attempt to fill the vacuum in their own being created by their inability or failure to fulfill the need of their mind for knowledge. This is the reason why there is so much unhappiness on earth. This is the reason why peace on earth never comes.

This essential relationship between knowledge and the mind is, in some sense, both good and bad. It is good because it obviously hastens mental growth which is essential to man's evolution. It is, however, bad and even dangerous in the sense that there is a great danger that it can be misled by the legion of false doctrines and dogmas out there masquerading as knowledge that can and do wreck havoc in one's life. Hence, the crucial significance to human life of discrimination: the ability to judge what is genuine and what is not. I do not know about others, but for me, there is only one true litmus test of what is true knowledge. That test is experience. If you have not experienced a thing, you have no knowledge of that thing. At best, you only have what in legal parlance is called hearsay or in common language is called rumor or gossip. And if you go around spreading it, you will be guilty of deception or telling a lie. Why? Because a lie is a discrepancy between what one knows or does not know and what one says. Or in other words, a lie is a disagreement between the mind and the speech. Some graphic examples are the following: if one knows that something is black and says that it is white, that is a lie. If one does not know something, because he does not have experience of it, and tells people about it as though he has knowledge of it, that also is a lie. The first example is obvious for a lot of people. The second one, however, is not so obvious and, therefore, more easily committed and more people are misled by it than the first. An egregious example of this is the case of religious clergy whose favorite sport is telling people about God, the devil, heaven, and hell with such fervor and enthusiasm as though they have met God and the devil or have been to heaven or hell so that they know what they are talking about. In all these cases, there is a huge discrepancy between knowledge or lack of it and speech, which is the definition of a lie or falsehood. The inevitable conclusion from this narrative is that religion, which is based on mere beliefs but is paraded and disguised as knowledge, is basically a lie, an unadulterated falsehood which deserves to be condemned and should be condemned.

Perhaps, the real culprit in this crime against moral truth is the absence of proper understanding about knowledge, its real nature, so much so that knowledge is commonly mistaken by a lot of people, even so-called erudite ones, with rumor, gossip, and even belief or faith—especially religious belief. At this juncture, perhaps it is necessary to fill in some blanks in our knowledge regarding knowledge per se. We shall therefore go back to our college days and refresh our knowledge of epistemology: the study of knowledge as knowledge.

Knowledge is quite an elusive and thus a highly interesting but frustrating subject. This is one of the subjects which we think we know until asked about it. Philosophers since ancient time up to the present have not found a common agreement regarding some of its salient issues, like the egregious universal. This fact is also exemplified by the different definitions which *Webster's Dictionary* has on this word. Be that as it may, we shall elucidate this controversial subject by taking a simplified but realistic approach on the subject to satisfy both philosophers and lay people. Surprisingly, *Webster's* initial definition of knowledge coincides with this approach. We shall therefore make use of this definition of knowledge in the lexicon as a jumping board, so to speak, in our discussion. *Webster* defines *knowledge* as "the fact or condition of knowing something with familiarity gained through experience or association." The significant words in this definition are "gained through experience."30 Let us follow this clue and analyze our experience when we undergo the process of knowing and achieve what we call knowledge or when we are said to know something. When we know a rose flower, for example, what actually happens? First, we see the rose and are attracted by its brilliant red color. Then when we touch it, we note its exquisite soft petals. And as we bring the rose close to our face, our sense of smell is rewarded with its sweet unique fragrance. If we are adventurous enough and nibble some of its petals, we note its peculiar taste. Note well that all these observations about the rose flower are the result of the rose impinging on our four senses of sight, touch, smell, and taste. In other words, in that brief encounter between the rose and our four senses, an intimate interaction or intercourse was established between them which made possible our gaining sensible information about the rose. To put it another way, in that moment of encounter or embrace, if you will, between the rose and our four senses, the rose and our four senses became one: a special kind of unity, a mysterious one, is created between them. This unity enables us to gain all those information about the rose: its color, texture, smell, and taste. These information are what we call our "sensible knowledge" about the rose. (We will skip the much debatable issue of whether we really have knowledge of the rose and not just its sensible qualities of color, smell, etc.)

Now, let us analyze in terms of knowledge what happened when we encountered the rose. Obviously, this encounter has three major players: (1) we, the knower, (2) the known (the rose), and (3) our knowledge of the rose. From the preceding analysis, we can now define knowledge as the result of the union between the knower and the known through experience (the encounter). Thus, the blessed trinity of knower, known, and knowledge makes possible the existence of human cognition. Without these three major players, there can be no human cognition. But note well that this drama of human cognition can be played only in the concrete stage of human experience. In other words, concrete experience is the basis of all knowledge. The clever Jesuits have distilled this principle in this Latin dictum I learned in college: "Quidquid est in intellectu prius fuerit in sensibus" (Whatever is in the intellect was first in the senses). In other words, all intellectual knowledge is based on sensible knowledge, knowledge gained through experience. In philosophical parlance, this is what is called empirical knowledge.

This definition of knowledge which is derived from experience is so significant to us humans that we seem to have a natural instinct for real knowledge so much so that any so-called knowledge which is not a product of our experience has practically no meaning for us. It has no real impact on our being.31 It does not grab us, so to speak. This is the reason why people keep on changing their religion because they cannot find the knowledge they are looking for in any religion. Poor people! They are simply unaware that religion does not and cannot teach real knowledge but only beliefs. They are also not aware that belief is not knowledge, that there is a world of difference between belief and knowledge, as explained earlier. It is therefore a colossal mistake to confuse knowledge with belief and vice versa. To show you the absolute futility of belief, I will give you a graphic example: if you are hungry and believe that there is food in the kitchen and just be satisfied with your belief and do not go to the kitchen and eat the food, you will remain hungry. You have to go beyond your belief, go to the kitchen and eat the food (if there is really food). Then and only then, you will be satisfied with the food because it is only then that the food and you become one when you eat it. Similarly, when you simply believe in God, as religion teaches, but do not know God, your belief is useless. You will always be "hungry" for God. This is the sorry fate of a lot of people who were fooled by religion to merely believe in God. No wonder people keep on changing their religion, hoping against hope that their new religion will satisfy their need for God only to be disappointed again and again.

Note well that experience plays a major and essential role in the never-ending drama of human knowledge. As previously mentioned, it is in the unique setting of experience that the dramatic encounter happened between the knower and the known which produced knowledge. Without the essential ingredient of experience, the delicious wonderful food of the mind which is knowledge cannot come into being. Hence, real knowledge is experiential knowledge. In this light, the result of deduction, which is merely a reasoning process, cannot be called knowledge, strictly speaking. Deduction is a result of the intellectual activity of the mind putting two and two together after it has acquired the knowledge of so many two's through experience of multiple concrete objects. This is the reason behind the popular dictum: experience is the best teacher. Indeed, experience is man's first and last teacher from cradle to grave and in between. Hence, experience is really man's best teacher. The knowledge found in man's intellect had its roots and beginning in man's experience by means of his senses. This is the basic doctrine of the philosophical movement called empiricism spearheaded by the British philosopher John Locke who strongly asserted that all knowledge comes from the senses, that all knowledge begins with experience. It is Locke who enriched philosophy with the theory that the mind is a tabula rasa, a blank tablet which throughout a man's lifetime would eventually be filled with the writing of experiential knowledge.[32]

Moreover, with regard to truth, it is only through our knowledge gained through experience that we can be sure of having truth in the sense of conformity of our knowledge with reality. Truth, in this sense, is difficult to come by because our senses, through which our mind acquires knowledge, suffer from terrible imperfections so much so that many of our so-called knowledge also suffer from the same defects. An obvious example is our common knowledge, based from our common experience, that the apple we are eating, for instance, is a solid object. However, science tells us that our common experience in this regard is totally wrong. An apple is made up of atoms, and as such, it is porous, not solid, because atoms are porous not solid. Why? Because as science tells us, an atom is made up of protons, electrons, and neutrons, which are points of energies moving around in empty space composing the atom. Hence, there are really no solid physical objects. Therefore, our experience of the apple, and every physical object for that matter, as solid is, at best, an illusion. Now, if we cannot even trust our personal experience to give us the truth about our knowledge of the apple, how can we trust other means of acquiring knowledge? How can we trust, for example, the experience of other people if we cannot even trust our own experience? How can we trust religion which is based on mere hearsay? That is how difficult to know truth in this relative world of ours. No wonder when Pilate asked Jesus what is truth, Jesus's answer was an eloquent silence.

We will not go into a labyrinthine discussion of the other theory of knowledge espoused by the school of thought called rationalists and their assumption of innate ideas, which made them conclude that not all knowledge comes from experience but that humans are already born with these innate ideas. The answer to this is simply that man's experience is not limited to a single lifetime, that man's experience encompasses a multitude of unimaginable lifetimes. Thus, man's knowledge from his previous lifetimes explains why he has innate ideas that nevertheless came from his previous experience in his previous lifetimes. This is the doctrine of reincarnation of which neither the empiricists nor the rationalists have any idea, which explains their myopic philosophical theories. Nonetheless, it is a doctrine which explains and sheds a lot of light on mysterious things in human life, including the innate ideas of the rationalists which they posited but cannot fully explain.

Speaking of reincarnation, this doctrine throws in bold relief the momentous significance of experience in human life. The ultimate reason behind reincarnation, why man has to be reborn over and over and thus be a hostage to the seemingly endless cycle of birth and death is experience. Experience is the only way, and perhaps the best way, by which man can achieve perfection in accordance with the universal law of universal evolution. And the only way for man to acquire enough experience to achieve that goal is through multiple reincarnation.33 This truth is enshrined in the doctrines of almost all the ancient religions of the world, including Judaism which gave birth to Christianity. A slight perusal of the Bible, especially the New Testament, will show this all too clearly. But of course, the Catholic Church does not adhere to the doctrine of reincarnation. Why? Because the Church is essentially a pagan religion.

Anyway, this is not the time and place to discuss reincarnation in depth. There is already a plethora of literature on this subject. Just visit the internet. I mentioned reincarnation only to highlight the all-important role experience plays in man's pursuit of knowledge and acquisition of perfection eventually. The meaningful corollary of this discussion on knowledge is that there is nothing to fear when it comes to experience since ultimately, the purpose of life is to experience. Thus, go on and experience life to the full without any fear or regret of anything. For there is really nothing to fear in life, not even fear itself. There is no success. There is no failure. There is only experience. And there is no such thing as good or bad experience. There is only experience. So go on and explore all the gamut of experience: all its ups and downs, its nooks and crannies, its light and darkness, its laughter and tears, its joys and sorrows. Scale all the depths and heights of experience. Leave no stone unturned in your quest for experience. Explore its agony and ecstasy, its heaven and hell, until there seems to be nothing more to experience.

But then do not rush into it. You have all eternity to do it. So relax and take your time. Take your sweet time to experience all the big and small things in life. For in the final analysis, there is really no such thing as big and small in life. There is only experience. So take time to live life fully in the fullness of your being through experience. Take time to surrender your being to the being of the present. This means appreciating the things and objects around you in full awareness with your senses. It means touching the objects around you with full attention. Notice that as you touch them, each object responds individually and uniquely to the magic of your touch. Notice that as you caress each object with your fingers, it suddenly becomes alive, for it is really alive, and caress your fingers in return and in gratitude for the precious attention you are giving it. Then suddenly, you become pleasantly aware that everything is alive and conscious and loves to be noticed and be given your gift of touch.

Then look closely at each object around you. In the stillness of your silent presence together with theirs, notice the individual impact of their being. Allow the magic of your being to fascinate their own and notice how they respond to yours. Then watch closely how in this mystical encounter of beings, the miracle and mystery of existence slowly and sweetly dawns on your consciousness. Then for the first time, you enjoy with gratitude the unspeakable bliss that comes to your soul in this moment of liberation from time as it is given a glimpse of eternity. Then suddenly, blissful tears flow unbidden from your grateful eyes.

Then listen to Being. Listen to Absolute: the infinite potential, the ineffable Nothing from which everything comes and goes. Listen to it in the silence that waits between gaps of every sound you hear. Listen to it in the rustling of the bamboo leaves, in the breaking of the waves on the shore, in the love song of the crickets at night. Listen to it in the stillness that punctuates every bird song, that counts every drops of the falling rain. Listen to it in the dramatic suspense that interrupts the deafening claps of thunder and the blinding flash of lightning. Listen to it in the blooming of love when lovers are alone and out of sight, when silence listens to their moans and sighs while the full moon is watching from the sky. Listen to it in the laughter of children at play, in the compelling sound of a baby's cry, and the haunting melody of a mother's lullaby. Listen to it in the voiceless plea of a beggar's outstretched hand and the hurried steps of the non-caring passersby. Listen to it in the hollow laughter of the rich enjoying their empty pleasures of the night. But never miss to listen to it in the stifled agony of a poor suffering on his deathbed. And finally, listen to it in the inaudible cadence of the beating of your heart when your mind finally transcends itself when it enters that realm of unbounded awareness and gives you a taste of nothing less than the Absolute. Then all of a sudden, you are free, free from the slavery and tyranny of the monster that is your own mind which snatches you willy-nilly from your transcendental embrace with the eternal present and locks you away within the time-bound confines of the past and the future.

Also, take time to be aware of Nothingness which embraces everything. And so, be aware of the empty space around you, that vast emptiness with which Nothingness garbs itself and everything else in creation. Before, you take notice of objects. This time, notice also the empty space that surrounds the objects because it is really the space that gives meaning and existence to them. And if you are lucky, you might realize—as science finally does—that reality, that everything is not only clothed with but is also made up of emptiness. Then you might realize that your very own body is simply a field of vast emptiness and that you yourself is nothing else but nothing as everything else.

To experience life fully, then, is a humbling experience. Before, you are living in a dream of your grandeur. Now, you wake up to the reality that you are Nothing.

But then, to experience life fully is also an enlightening process. Indeed, you wake up to the reality that you are nothing. But at the same time, you also wake up to the reality that everything else is also nothing, and therefore, you are one with the wonderful world of Nothingness, one with the void ocean of consciousness, one with the totality of Being.

In sum, to experience life fully is to die to your illusory self and be born again to your real Self. When that miracle happens, you will know the meaning of Christ's words: "Know the truth and the truth shall set you free."

Chapter

9

Sex and Happiness

Love makes the world go around, according to common belief. As expected of common belief, that is not true. There is a force more basic, more primordial, more powerful than love. This force makes the world not only turn around but even go upside down. Love has become so ordinary, prosaic, and commonplace that it no longer attracts attention. But this force I am referring to is so exciting, enthralling, and provocative that by the very mention of its name, eyes open wide, heads turn around, mouths salivate, and other organs of the body I need not mention immediately and unconsciously respond. That is the awesome power of this awesome force.

Sex is this force—as you have guessed correctly. The compelling strength of this force is not just fearsome. It is terrifying. I tremble to imagine how it so dominates the entire being of all the rapists that they, oblivious of everything else even of their safety and life, would violate the person and being of their hapless victim and also put themselves in danger. For what? Only for the brief and fleeting satisfaction of their sexual need. However, there is a beautiful side to this terrifying force. It can bring to the pinnacle of transcendental bliss the blessed lovers who surrender to its irresistible sway so much so that their sexual experience is nothing less than a glimpse of what religion calls beatific vision, a foretaste of the absolute.

But why is the character of this force called sex so contradictory that it has become an absolute conundrum? It is simply because, like any other force, sex can be an instrument either for good or its opposite. In order to deal effectively with sex, it is therefore imperative that we take an impassioned look at it and try to understand its real nature. Let us start with the definition of sex. Our friend *Webster* defines sex as "the sum of the structural, functional, and behavioral characteristics of organisms that are involved in reproduction marked by the union of gametes, and that distinguish males and females."34 I find this definition of sex not only lengthy but rather too restrictive, conservative, and exclusive. I shall propose a brief, simplified, and inclusive definition of sex that will conform to our umbrella concept of sex. Here it is: SEX is Symbiotic Energy Xchange. How does that definition of sex grab you? It is not only simple, brief, easily understood, and remembered because it turned sex into an acronym, but also includes all aspects of sex, except perhaps what we call solitary sex. But solitary sex is not a problem, except of course for the moral fanatics and fundamentalists who consider solitary sex as an abnormality and moral abomination. But their distorted opinion does not really count. So our definition is on the right track philosophically and scientifically. Solitary sex is simply the exception to the rule but ironically, the most practiced. Let us, therefore, take a closer look at our definition of sex and find out how it conforms to the philosophical and scientific paradigm of sex.

As mentioned earlier, sex is nature's way of preserving itself by preserving all the organisms that compose nature. And nature does this through symbiotic energy exchange (sex) among organisms. Hence, sex is nature's unique way of addressing effectively the all-important and paramount issue of survival. Since survival is the first and fundamental law of life, sex also essentially shares with and is governed by this primordial principle. This explains the unspeakable supreme power of sex since life is the most powerful principle or energy in nature. This explains the overpowering madness that engulfs and overwhelms a rapist, as mentioned earlier. This explains the reported spontaneous combustion that sometimes happens in the house of a family who has a teenage daughter whose blooming sexuality is so strong that it is transformed into fire that suddenly comes from nowhere. This explains the phenomenon which unenlightened society calls sexual perversions that are merely expressions of the powerful energy of sex demanding to be expressed within the exigencies of the moment. This explains the pathological fear of sex by religious fundamentalists, a fear which found its culmination during the infamous Inquisition by demonizing sex and burning at the stakes in public view those suspected by the Catholic Church of practicing unnatural sex. This explains the homophobic aberration of people in all ages including our present era.

Take note that sex is a symbiotic act. Hence, it is a form of symbiosis which etymologically means the coming together (sym) of living things (bios). Sex, therefore, entails "intercourse." This means that a sexual act, by its definition, is a social activity involving, of course, at least two participants. Hence, masturbation, a usual solitary act, strictly speaking, is not a sexual act. In this context, it is better defined as a "pleasurable stimulation of one's sexual organ." However, for simplicity, we shall include masturbation within a larger concept of sex. Now, what about mutual masturbation, does it fall within the strict definition of sexual act? Also, within the context of our definition of sex as a symbiotic act, the phrase "sexual intercourse" is a tautology since the meaning of "intercourse" is already included in the meaning of the word "sexual."

The fact that sex normally involves intercourse explains why for most people, the author included, a normal sexual activity—sex between two people, at least—is most pleasurable. Hence, it is mostly practiced by the majority of humans. This also explains why different sexual activities such as vaginal sex, anal sex, oral sex, femoral sex, involve two people, at least.

Also take note that our definition of sex implies that it is an activity that may be performed not necessarily by persons of opposite sex. Hence, the sexual activities of homosexuals, bisexuals, transgenders, and what have you, as long as they are done at least in pairs, fall within the ambit of our definition of sex.

Take note further that our definition of sex is not exclusive of humans but inclusive of animals as well as plants. In other words, our definition of sex is all-embracing and nature oriented. It includes all the natural players of creation that propagate their species through symbiotic energy exchange.

Ironically, a symbiotic energy exchange does not necessarily result in procreation. This is extremely important since it impacts many of the controversial issues that bedevil our society today such as same-sex marriage. This is true even in sexual intercourse between opposite sex intended by both partners for procreation. It does not always result in pregnancy and pregnancy does not always result in giving birth. Hence, since even nature itself does not intend sex to be done exclusively for procreation, it does not stand to reason and it is against nature to say that sex done for pleasure and not for procreation—such as coitus interruptus, oral and anal sex, etc.—is contrary to nature or unnatural and therefore condemnable. A contrary view is best refuted by the innumerable controversies it spawns.

There are several significant insights to be derived from the above discussion. First and foremost is the fact that nature is liberal with regard to sex. Nature does not really care if sexual activity results in procreation or not. This is very significant in the present context in which population explosion is a serious world problem. In fact, nature herself provides her own solutions to this problem by creating automatic sexual safety valves in the form of homosexuals, celibates, barren women, and impotent men, among others. This clearly shows the supreme wisdom of nature.

Secondly, nature is extremely generous in dispensing sexual pleasure especially to humans. While the sexual activities of plants and animals are strictly regulated by nature so that their sexual activities are seasonal, the sexual activities of humans know no time and season and are left entirely by nature to human free will so much so that humans engage in sex anytime they want and as often as they want. Whereas plants and animals have only limited ways to express their sexuality, human's sexual expressions are limited only by their fecund imagination and creativity.

Thirdly, all sexual activities found in nature are regulated by nature itself in accordance with the instinctual, natural law of gratification. This is what is called in Freudian parlance the "pleasure principle." Thus, all forms of sexual gratification are natural in the sense that they are natural offshoots of the natural primordial tendency of man who is part and parcel of nature. In this sense, although the sexual activities of humans are freely done, basically, they are still regulated by nature. Hence, the conclusion that all sexual activities of humans are natural and, therefore, there is no such thing as unnatural sex is inevitable and incontrovertible.

Fourth, since sex is essentially energy, the only rational way of dealing with sex is to treat it as energy. Experience tells us that energy in any form cannot be suppressed. It can be transformed, transmuted, or channeled but never suppressed. Ignorance or violation of this natural law results in dire psychological consequences that made Freud famous for having discovered them. Moreover, attempts to suppress sexual tendencies considered sinful by wearing hair shirts or flagellation—as practiced by ignorant religious people during the Middle Ages and even today—only results in unnecessary suffering for the human body. Furthermore, suppression of sexual energy, such as the erroneous practice of celibacy by Catholic priests and nuns only results in the shocking and expensive scandals by pedophile Catholic priests. All these unfortunate cases only prove that one cannot violate nature with impunity.

Fifth, sex, particularly the type of sex which results in procreation, is wise nature's way of addressing in one supreme stroke the supreme issues of preserving the human species as well as the need of the spirit to experience its absolute nature. Hence, through sex, nature is hitting two birds in one stone, in a manner of speaking, as you will find out from the following paragraphs.

What we have covered so far are the physical and psychological dimensions of sex. These are the sexual topics most people are interested in and knowledgeable of. But these are only the tip of the iceberg that is sex. We shall now discuss the submerged part of the sexual iceberg which is the spiritual dimension of sex. Let us start with what people enjoy most about sex: orgasm. Orgasm is the culmination of sexual experience. It is the alpha and omega of sexual activity. From its very start until its very end, sexual activity, or lovemaking if you will, is focused on orgasm. If something happens that orgasm is not achieved, the entire sexual exercise is a dismal failure and the whole day is ruined. But if orgasm is achieved, then heaven flings wide its open door and the whole day is blessed. Such is the awesome magic of orgasm. But why is orgasm such a magical experience? What is its enchanting secret?

The answer lies in the esoteric fact that orgasm is not so much an intensely pleasurable experience as a mystical spiritual epiphany. The entire sexual exercise leading to orgasm is transcendental meditation in disguise. The awesome similarity between sex and meditation is absolutely intriguing. In sex, as in meditation, one starts with ablution. When sexual encounter and meditation finally starts, one's attention is initially focused on the object of pleasure or bliss since pleasure or bliss is the mind's ultimate objective. Then little by little and ever so slowly, in sex as in meditation, one's consciousness loses its connection with the physical surrounding and is focused exclusively on the activity of the moment until that magical state is reached when one falls into the unspeakable abyss of nothingness and explodes into the primordial ecstasy of the orgasmic big bang. In that fleeting moment, one's mind transcends itself and zooms into a thoughtless state of pure unbounded awareness. In that mystical moment, one's consciousness has broken into the barrier of relativity and emerges within the dimension of the Absolute. In that mystical moment, one has died to his illusory self and reborn to his divine real Self in the Kingdom of God. This is what Christ meant when he told Nicodemus: "Most assuredly I say to you unless one is born again he cannot see the kingdom of God" (John 3:3). This is the nirvana of Buddhism. This is the satori of Zen Buddhism. This is the ultimate experience of the Spanish mystic Juan de la Cruz when he soars into heavenly ecstasy, the experience he sighs and longs for in his agony during his "dark night of the soul" when he can no longer experience his spiritual "orgasm" because he does not know how to practice transcendental meditation and he does not engage in sex because he is a monk.

In other words, what makes orgasm so amazingly attractive and powerfully enchanting is not so much orgasm per se but the spiritual effect of orgasm. To be sure, orgasm completely satisfies the physical and emotional needs of humans. But humans are not simply physical and emotional beings. Humans are mental and spiritual beings as well. And it goes without saying that the mental and spiritual components of humans have also their own proper needs demanding to be satisfied properly. And for some people, those highly evolved souls, the needs of their mind and spirit are more compelling than their bodily needs. The paramount question, therefore, is how should the mental and spiritual needs of humans be satisfied and fulfilled? For the majority of humans who do not practice spiritual exercises, the only way they derive spiritual satisfaction is through the experience of the spiritual effect of orgasm as previously explained. This explains why sex, aside from food, dominates the consciousness and behavior of humans. Because of this, enterprising individuals have become master purveyors of sex. They make use of sex to sell almost anything— from cars to medicine—by means of the powerful psychological tool called association of ideas. They manipulate people's mind to buy things by associating them with sex. Through this marketing gimmick, when people buy things, they also buy sex without their knowing it. This is another proof of the amazing power of sex because of its spiritual component.

Let us now address an important issue regarding sex which is not properly addressed. That issue is celibacy. It is a discipline imposed by the Catholic Church to its clerics who are required to take a vow of celibacy when they are ordained. Hence, Catholic priests are not supposed to marry and should refrain from any sexual activity. But do they? It is a common knowledge that celibacy has produced four kinds of priests. The first kind consists of those who are truly celibate, who are able to live up to their vow of celibacy. Knowing human nature, you can be sure that these priests are either extinct or belong to the endangered species. The second kind consists of those priests who found out that they made a terrible mistake of becoming priests. To properly remedy their mistake, they petition the Vatican for dispensation so they can get married and live a layman's life. These are the honest priests. In fairness to the Catholic Church, the number of these honest priests is considerable. To the third kind belong those who want to follow the example of those who belong to the second kind but are terrified by the not so attractive prospect of living an ordinary life of having to earn one's bread from the sweat of one's brow. And they are absolutely right! Life in the world as an ordinary man is not easy. The life of a priest who does not have to stretch a muscle and yet still get a financial windfall from donations of generous parishioners is far more attractive. So these practical priests choose to remain being priests and at the same time support a family. Actually, it is a good choice practically speaking since they have the best of both worlds. But these are the dishonest priests. They go through the difficult process of trying to hide from their parishioners the fact that they have wives and families while continuing to perform their priestly functions of saying mass, hearing confessions, etc. But as expected, their double life is an open secret to their parishioners who simply shrug their shoulders and say, "Boys will always be boys." Of course, the Vatican is also aware of the existence of these dishonest priests. But what can Vatican do? The number of these priests is legion. If they are removed from the Church, the Church will have to close shop. And the Church will never let that happen. And so, on this issue of dishonest priests, the Vatican wisely adopts the policy of choosing the lesser evil. Indeed, it is a wise policy! Thus, the Catholic Church still ranks as the biggest church or religion on this planet. The fourth kind consists of different kind of boys. They love other boys. They are the pedophile priests who are giving the Vatican a lot of legal and financial problems. I do not have to elaborate on this critical issue. The media has already done a better job.

Indeed, celibacy is a huge issue in the Catholic Church. The history of the Church shows that this issue has been a pain in the neck, so to speak, for ages. The reason why the Church is not able to address this issue is the wrong perception by the Church of the natural component of human nature called sex—a wrong perception which over time has metamorphosed into a pathological attitude about sex. This is the reason behind many of the erroneous and even ludicrous Catholic doctrines involving sex.

Take for instance the Church's doctrine of virgin birth. The Church teaches that Jesus was divine: the second person of the Blessed Trinity. Hence, Jesus cannot be born of a human father but of a divine Father. Hence, the Church teaches that Jesus was conceived by the Holy Spirit, the third person of the Blessed Trinity, and was born by a virgin called Mary. This means that Joseph, the husband of Mary, has nothing to do with the conception and birth of Jesus. In graphic terms, this means that Jesus was not conceived through sexual intercourse between Joseph and Mary. In other words, Jesus is a product of asexual reproduction or parthenogenesis which etymologically means: "Parthenos" (virgin) and "genesis" (birth). According to science, parthenogenesis as a natural phenomenon occurs only in plants and animals. Theoretically, it can also occur in humans. But it never did. There is no documented single occurrence of natural parthenogenesis in the whole of human history. A real human parthenogenesis, according to Wikipedia, occurred in August 2, 2007, when a South Korean scientist, Hwang Woo-Suk, accidentally created the first human embryo through parthenogenesis. But this is not natural parthenogenesis. It is artificial. It happened in the laboratory of a scientist, not in a human womb. Hence, I repeat, there is no documented case of a woman in the entire human history who ever conceived a child through asexual reproduction or parthenogenesis. All stories about virgin birth, women conceiving asexually, are just that—stories and nothing more. And there are so many of these stories of virgin birth that even antedated the story of Jesus's virgin birth. Some of these stories involve famous legendary personalities like Horus, Buddha, Lao-tse, Dionysus, Krishna, Hercules, Mithra, and many more whose births, like that of Jesus, were accordingly of supernatural origin. Hence, it is arguably true that the story of Jesus's virgin birth is copied from these previous stories.

Another objection against Jesus's so-called virgin birth is the surprising fact that the very same gospel which says that Jesus's father is the Holy Spirit also says that Joseph is Jesus's father. Hence, there is an obvious contradiction here that must be resolved. Luke 1:26–36 narrates the incidence where the angel Gabriel told Mary that she will conceive a son through the Holy Spirit and he will be called Jesus. The Church calls this incidence the Annunciation. However, Luke 3:23–38 is about the genealogy of Jesus which narrates that Jesus came from the bloodline of David through Jesus's father Joseph who is of David's bloodline. Now, which is which? Is the Holy Spirit the father of Jesus as told by the angel Gabriel to Mary as narrated in Luke 1:26–36, or is it Joseph as stated in the account of Jesus's genealogy as narrated in Luke 3:23–38? Perhaps they are both true since there is no contradiction if we assume that Jesus was conceived by the Holy Spirit through the instrumentality of Joseph. But this theory of mine does not sit well with the Catholic Church because it does not dovetail with the meaning of the virgin birth of Jesus. But my point is: what is the whole point of the doctrine of virgin birth? Why should the Church go to such trouble of fabricating a fantastic story about the virgin birth of Jesus when a natural story that his father was Joseph can serve as well and even better since it is in perfect consonant with Jesus's genealogy? The reason, as pointed out earlier, is the Church's pathological erroneous attitude about sex. Jesus, the man-God redeemer of mankind, cannot and should not be born by means of sexual intercourse. Hence, the story of the virgin birth was fabricated, a story which was proven to be a lie by the Gospel itself, not only by the Gospel of Luke, as pointed out, but also by the Gospel of Matthew 1:1–16 which is the account of Christ's genealogy as the son of David through Joseph also the son of David. This shows that crime does not really pay, even if the crime is committed by the Catholic Church. This also shows that truth also comes out no matter what—as Christ correctly said.

Another example of a Church's teaching which does not even have a scriptural basis and therefore was fabricated again by the Church in accordance with its pathological aversion of sex is that Christ never married and is therefore celibate. Several books have been written to refute this baseless claim by the Church. The most popular, of course, is Dan Brown's best seller, *The Da Vinci Code*. It was so popular that it was made into a movie. I read the book, and I also saw the movie. If I am not mistaken, this novel of Dan Brown became so popular because it was condemned by the Church for disseminating false information about Jesus's sexuality. (I hope the Church will do the same to my book.) But there is another book which I found more credible than *The Da Vinci Code* because it is not a fiction and is backed and supported by historical facts. That book is *Holy Blood, Holy Grail*. The book's thesis is that the Holy Grail is really Mary Magdalene (the wife of Jesus) who contained in her womb the Holy Blood (child) of Jesus. The authors proved their thesis by showing that Jesus survived the crucifixion—Christ did not really die since he was resuscitated by his followers after the crucifixion—escaped to Europe with Mary Magdalene, and raised a family there.

I cannot understand why the Catholic Church teaches that Jesus Christ is celibate and unmarried. There is no direct evidence in the Gospels about the status of Jesus Christ. But according to the authors of *Holy Blood, Holy Grail*, there are many circumstantial evidences in the Gospels pointing to the fact that Jesus is married to Mary Magdalene. One of these is the fact that the first person whom Jesus visited after he rose from the dead is Mary Magdalene, not his mother Mary, nor his beloved disciple John, but Mary Magdalene. This fact makes sense only if Jesus has an intimate relation with Mary Magdalene, the relation of husband and wife.

Besides, what is wrong if Jesus is married? According to the teaching of the Church, Jesus is true God and true man. If so, the fact that Jesus is married simply dovetails with the teaching of the Church that Jesus is true man, indeed. And a normal man, at that. Otherwise, it would be difficult, if not impossible, for us ordinary humans to identify with him and imitate his life and follow his teachings, all of which the Church is teaching us to do but preventing us from doing by teaching erroneously that Christ is divine and as such lived an abnormal celibate life.

All of the above simply proves that the Catholic Church has no inkling about the true nature and momentous significance of sex and has a distorted notion of celibacy which is a natural function of human sexuality raised to a spiritual level. We shall therefore devote the last part of this chapter on this ticklish issue of celibacy. As previously mentioned, celibacy is a natural function of sex raised to a spiritual level. In other words, celibacy is a natural effect of spiritual life and not the other around. Hence, celibacy should not be used as a *means* to achieve a spiritual life—as the Church is doing. Rather, it should be seen as an *end* or result of a genuine spiritual life. Let me explain.

Ordinary humans experience the spiritual component of their being through orgasm, the culmination of the sexual act. That is why for ordinary people, sex is a bodily, emotional, and spiritual necessity for their happiness—as previously explained. But whether we like it or not, we humans are not born equal. There are among us old or advance souls whose spiritual life is on such a lofty level that for them, the spiritual experience of orgasm is no longer satisfactory. Perhaps, their lofty spiritual life is a by-product of their previous reincarnation. Or presently, they have tasted a more satisfying spiritual experience— through meditation, perhaps—so much so that they are totally weaned from sex and so celibacy comes naturally for them. Also, they find out that the practice of celibacy enhances their spiritual practice and thus their spiritual life as well. In other words, unknowingly, they are able to convert or transmute their sexual energy to spiritual energy in the same manner that an engineer can convert the energy of flowing water to electrical energy. Thus, these lucky souls have no more need to experience orgasm since they have found a more satisfying spiritual experience. This phenomenon is commonplace in human life. Its dynamics is the same as a child who no longer wants to breastfeed because it has experienced a better tasting food, or a beer-drinking man who no longer wants to drink beer because he has tasted the more pleasurable cognac, or a cigarette-smoking guy whose addiction to cigarette disappeared because he is now addicted to smoking cannabis. The litany is endless. This, in brief, is the dynamics of celibacy. I repeat, celibacy is a natural by-product of a lofty spiritual life. If you are advanced spiritually, celibacy will be practiced by you naturally. You do not have to make a vow of celibacy. But no matter how many vows of celibacy you will make, if you are not spiritually ready for celibacy, the more you will want to have sex. This is the principle of what is prohibited becomes more attractive. There will be a war within you: a war between nature which urges you to have sex versus your vow to practice celibacy. Of course, nature will win, as it always does. Then willy-nilly, you will have to break your vow in order to enjoy sex. This is the ordeal those poor Catholic priests and nuns have to go through because they are not ready for this lofty spiritual practice of celibacy. Their vow of celibacy is a pure exercise in futility and misery. As Nietzsche aptly said, "Those for whom chastity is difficult should be counseled against it, lest it become their road to hell —the mud and heat of their souls."[35]

To recap, sex is symbiotic energy exchange. The mutual sharing of this natural energy gives humans, animals, and plants the immense pleasure they need not only for their individual well-being but for the growth and survival of their species as well. Hence, sex is necessary for their individual and collective happiness. From the nature of sex, the following conclusions inevitably follow: (1) All forms of sexual activity are natural. (2) Sex is intended by nature for pleasure or procreation or both. (3) Sex as energy demands that it should not be suppressed but may be converted or transformed to spiritual energy. (4) Celibacy, the abstinence from sex, should be the natural result of spiritual perfection. To practice celibacy for the purpose of attaining spiritual perfection, as being done by priests and nuns, is a huge mistake resulting in a huge suffering.

Now that you know the nature and dynamics of sex, you can enjoy it more. Have a good time.

10

Love and Happiness

Is love essential to happiness? Can a person not be happy without falling in love or without loving anybody? Since the normal trajectory of human life seems to include falling in love, a book on the philosophy of human happiness will not be complete without addressing this primordial issue of love. Hence, our initial queries on love vis-à-vis happiness should be addressed properly.

We have seen that happiness is the satisfaction or fulfillment of human needs. In order for love therefore to be essential to happiness, love has to fulfill a human need. But does it? Do humans need to fall in love? Or do humans merely think they have to fall in love, and therefore, they eventually fall in love? Is falling in love therefore a mere self-deception practiced by humans? Is the idea then of falling in love simply one of those Jungian archetypes that humans develop in the long course of human evolution and therefore has really nothing to do with basic human needs? To answer truthfully these fundamental questions, we have to again make use of our methodology of defining things and ideas, and therefore, we have to define "love" initially in order to have a clear idea of its nature.

The lexicon has a long definition of love which extends from love of one's child to love of God. However, it has this definition of love which we can use as a working definition: love is a "strong affection for another arising out of kinship or personal ties." The significant words in this definition are "affection for another." What in reality does this "affection" consist of? Since affection has to do with feelings or emotions, let us consult our feelings or emotions when we say we are in love. What do we really feel when we are in love? Don't we all feel we want to be "one" with the object of our love so that we kiss and embrace the person we love? These acts of kissing and embracing, are they not acts of trying to be one with the person we love? Absolutely! Since we are physically separated from the object of our love, we resort to doing acts that will somehow remove the gap of separation. Hence, kissing and embracing are acts of love. They somehow unite us with the objects of our love—although not quite. Hence, we keep on trying to discover ways and means to achieve the unity we desire. This explains the amazing and sometimes amusing techniques of lovemaking humans have discovered and developed throughout the ages, techniques that differ according to cultural differences. The most famous of these techniques are those invented by the Hindus, the Kama Sutra. Still, no matter what position or technique of lovemaking humans resort to, they cannot achieve the unity they are looking for. Why? The reason is quite obvious. There can be no perfect unity between material objects or bodies unless, perhaps, they are transformed into molecular or atomic level. Hence, knowing this, highly evolved souls find the perfect unity they are looking for in the realm of the spirit. They engage in the spiritual exercise of transcendental meditation in which they experience absolute unity with the Absolute within themselves, at the spiritual core of their being.

This brings us to another school of thought that teaches that man is a microcosm, a small universe. Hence, man is complete. Nobody has to fall in love with another in order to find the love, the unity he is looking for. Anybody can find that love, the unity within one's own being. This is the reason why throughout human history, there are always souls who live this kind of spiritual life. They have no need of falling in love with another since they found true love within themselves. Thus, they live a celibate life, not because they made a vow of celibacy, but because they have no need of sex to make them happy. In fact, for these lucky souls, sex is merely a hindrance on their journey to perfection. And so they simply channel their sexual energy to enhance their spiritual activities as well as their happiness.

In terms of psychology, this human desire to be united with the object of one's love is called identification. We identify with the object of our love. When we are in love, something strange happens to our mind. We think that we and our beloved are one. Love therefore is basically rooted in love of one's self. Love for others is essentially self-love. Thus, one cannot love another if one does not love one's self. This is why those who were deprived of love when they were young and, therefore, have not learned to love themselves turn out to be antisocial. These are the criminals, the enemies of society. They are unable to identify themselves with others and therefore incapable of loving. This is the real meaning of Christ's words: "Love your neighbor as you love yourself." It really means: as you love yourself, love your neighbor. It really means: our love for our neighbor is based on our love for ourselves. It really means: if we have no love for ourselves, we can have no love for our neighbor. The obvious corollary of all these is that contrary to the teaching of religion, self-love is not a vice. It is virtue. The highest virtue.

This explains the immense power of love. This explains why humans think nothing of dying for love, a favorite subject of writers throughout human history, thus producing great novels on love, romantic love poems, and sweet songs of love. I am referring to not only to the common love between man and a woman but to all the wide spectrum of love which includes parental love, friendly love, and even patriotic love to which society gives a medal or raises a monument. Apropos of this issue, maybe Nietzsche's view is relevant. He said, "A real man wants two things: danger and play. Therefore, he wants woman as the most dangerous plaything."36

However, this awesome power of love has a negative side to it. It can drive you crazy, literary, if unrequited. Forlorn lovers know only too well what I mean. I know because I am one of them. I almost lost my mind and committed suicide when it happened to me. It was then I realized the meaning of the phrase: "falling" in love. Only my strong mind and love for myself saved me from falling into the abyss of unrequited love. But then again, unrequited love has also a positive side to it, like the silver lining in a dark cloud. Unrequited love is also a favorite topic of romantic authors producing what the poet Shelley calls, "Our sweetest songs are those that tell of saddest thought."

Let us go to another topic about love which everybody talks about but hardly understands: love of God. Is there really such a thing? Can anybody really love God? Can humans who cannot even love a beautiful plant or a lovable animal or another fellow human, so much so that they think nothing of killing them, can they really love God whom they do not even know and not even sure he exists? This is one of the many conundrums of human life, a conundrum people do not even think about, let alone examine its mystery. As a final installment to this chapter on love, let us examine the dynamics of love vis-à-vis the religious commandment: "Love God."

As previously explained, love is the desire or the need to be one or be united with the beloved or the object of one's love. In mathematical form, love = lover + beloved. In this equation, the given factors are (1) lover, (2) beloved, and (3) knowledge by the lover of his beloved (represented by the + sign). As the law of equation demands, without any of these three factors that make one side of the equation, the other side of the equation (love) does not exist. However, there is an element in this equation on love which is often overlooked by humans because it is not fully understood. This is the essential element of knowledge by the lover of the beloved which joined them together. As previously stated, in our equation, this essential element is represented by the symbol +. In other words, in order for a "lover" to have "love," it is essential not only to have a "beloved" or object of love but to "know" that beloved or object of love; otherwise, there is no love.

Why is it essential for humans to know the object of their love in order for love to exist? It is because we humans are "knowing" beings. We are blessed with a mind (the faculty of knowing) and a brain (the organ of knowing). Hence, since we humans act and behave holistically (as one organism), with regard to love, we act, behave, and function not only in accordance with our feelings, but holistically, together with our knowing faculty. In fact, it is the human faculty of knowing which dictates on the human faculty of feeling on which love depends. This is especially true for people who are blessed with a superior mind. They cannot love somebody they do not admire and think highly of. Shakespeare's words, "Love is blind and lovers cannot see," are poetic hyperbole and therefore should not be taken literally. "Love is partially blind, and lovers are partially blinded" is much nearer to the truth on the matter of love. Like a gem, a person, no matter how excellent, has always some flaws that a partially blinded lover does not see. The lover sees only the brilliant qualities of the beloved. Nonetheless, the lover has to know the beloved in order to see these enchanting qualities. Thus, knowledge is absolutely an essential ingredient of love. Thus, one can love God only if one has knowledge of God. But how is this possible? How can one have knowledge of God in order to love God? How can one have knowledge of this supreme being whose existence we are not even sure of? This is the supreme problem about knowing this supreme being. Religion tells us to love this supreme being, but religion has no knowledge of this supreme being, knowledge that religion can share with us so that we can love this supreme being. All that religion has is faith and all what religion can do is tell us to believe that this supreme being exists. Even science is in the dark with regard to the existence of this supreme being. Science does not even want to touch this issue because it cannot prove the existence of this supreme being which is beyond the experience of the scientist. Philosophy fares no better. Immanuel Kant, one of the most brilliant German philosophers, says that God cannot be proven nor disproven. This means that God cannot be the proper subject of philosophy but only of religion. In other words, neither religion nor science nor philosophy can give us the knowledge of God we need in order to love God. No wonder, even Jesus Christ has no exhortation about loving God, but only about loving your neighbor as you love yourself.

However, the biggest irony about Christians on loving their neighbors is the fact that Christian history clearly shows that Christ's injunction to love one's neighbor is more honored in breach than in observance by so-called Christians by killing their fellow humans in the name of Christ as shown by the Inquisition and the Crusade and other religious wars in human history.

But granting for the sake of argument that there is God and that we know him, should we not therefore love God as we love our parents? The problem with this argument is that we have no obligation to love our parents. Why? Because the obligation to love our parents necessarily implies that there is a contract between our parents and ourselves, a quid pro quo contract which says that there is an agreement between our parents and ourselves that we love our parents in return for our parents giving us birth and caring for us in this life. Is there such a contract? Since the answer is in the negative, there is also a negative obligation that we love our parents. The fact is that all the obligation is on the part of our parents. They have the sole absolute obligation to love and care for us because they were solely responsible for bringing us in this world. This is what is called in legal parlance, a unilateral act. Therefore, if we love our parents, it is not a matter of obligation but a matter of choice on our part. We love our parents not because we *must* but because we *want to.*

The same is true for God. If God exists, our relationship with God is the same as our relationship with our parents. Thus, we have no obligation to love God, but God has the absolute obligation to love us. If we love God, it is for us not a matter of obligation but a matter of choice. This is the reason why Christ has no teaching that we should love God. His supreme teaching is to love our neighbor as we love ourselves. Why? Simply because there can be no peace on earth unless we follow this supreme law of love.

The Muslims have a more rational view of love vis-à-vis Allah, their God. They do not love Allah. They *fear* him. Thus, Koran, their holy book, is filled with exhortation about fearing Allah. To my mind, this is not only a rational view but a realistic one. Why? Simply because they do not know Allah. Hence, they fear him since fear should be the right approach concerning something or somebody you do not know, especially if that somebody is conceived or imagined to be all-powerful, all-knowing, but unknowable and mysterious as Allah.

Hence, Christians' so-called love for God is a mere illusion, to say the least. It is not even in harmony with the teaching of Jesus Christ who has no teaching about loving God but all about loving one's fellow man and loving one's enemies. If Christians really want to love God, then they should at least try to know God instead of just talking about loving God. But then, this is typical of Christians. They are contented and happy in mere illusions like faith or belief. They do not really care about knowledge of God. They were brainwashed by their religion that one can know God only in heaven if they go there after they die. The rational conclusion of this erroneous teaching is: why should one allow oneself to "suffer the arrows and slings of outrageous fortune" in this life, to quote Shakespeare, if one can be happy afterlife? One might as well end one's life.

In sum, in light of the foregoing, the answer to our initial question in this chapter is obviously in the affirmative. Oh yes, love is essential to happiness. Absolutely! You cannot be truly happy unless you truly love yourself. You will not be able to provide for the needs of your body, your mind, and your spirit—the essential components of your self—in order to make you happy, unless you love yourself.

However, the problem for us humans is *how* to love ourselves. Humans are generally unhappy because they do not really know the right way of loving themselves. Even the supposedly intellectually superior members of the human race: the geniuses, the philosophers, the scientists, etc., do not know the proper way of loving themselves, so much so that they turn out to be the unhappiest people on earth. This is one of the ironies and tragedies of the human race.

This is why this book is written: to fill up the abysmal ignorance of humans on the proper way of love so they will find happiness and so that peace on earth will finally dawn to give more happiness to humans.

Chapter

11

Emotions and Happiness

My *Merriam-Webster's Collegiate Dictionary* defines "emotion" as follows: "a conscious mental reaction (as anger or fear) subjectively experienced as strong feeling usually directed toward a specific object and typically accompanied by physiological and behavioral changes in the body." One cannot find a better definition of emotion than this. It also defines emotion in one word: feeling. Emotion and feeling are therefore synonymous. Hence, in this chapter, we shall use emotion and feeling interchangeably.

Now, what is the relationship between happiness and emotion? Happiness is the cause of delightful and pleasant human emotions such as joy, satisfaction, bliss, and other shades of positive emotions resulting from the fulfillment of human needs. On the flip side, unhappiness also causes negative emotions that tell us that there is a vacuum or vacuums in our being that need to be filled. Hence, it is essential that we understand the nature and dynamics of emotion for a better understanding, appreciation, and management of happiness or unhappiness.

We humans are so intimately connected with our emotions that there is no moment in our conscious life that we do not feel any emotion. Why this is so can perhaps be attributed to the fact that emotion is so essentially important in our well-being that not only our happiness but even our very own survival depends on how we relate and address our emotions. Take the emotion of fear, for instance. We all know that in the face of an enemy, there is only one thing that can save us, and that is the emotion of fear. It is fear that will compel us either to fight or take flight—depending on the circumstances—in order to survive. When we need food in order to live, it is the feeling of hunger that will compel us to find and take food to address properly this visceral need. And so on; the examples are innumerable. Indeed, every moment of our life, our constant inseparable companion in our journey is emotion. That is how vital and significant our emotion is in our life.

Emotion, therefore, is nature's way of taking care of the well- being of the whole human race and at the same time its own well- being.

But as everything else in this relative world where we live, there is a downside to this wonderful feeling called emotion. If we do not watch out, an emotion can be so powerful that it can overwhelm us to such an extent that we lose control of our self. Thus, instead of using emotion to our advantage, we allow emotion to use us to our own disadvantage and even destruction. Thus, emotion, instead of being an asset as nature intended it to be, becomes a deadly liability. An egregious common example of this is the case of a person who was so overwhelmed by the feeling of jealousy that after killing his wife and her suspected lover, he killed himself. Another one is the common case of a dejected lover who was overwhelmed with the emotion of despair that he committed suicide. Still, another common one is the case of person who was overwhelmed with the feeling of lust that he raped and killed his hapless victim. Indeed, the list of tragic cases caused by overwhelming emotions is endless.

It is, therefore, of paramount importance and extremely relevant to our happiness that we understand the nature and dynamics of emotion so that we should be able to use it for our well-being instead of allowing it to use us to our perdition.

There are many theories of emotion that attempt to explain the why and wherefore of emotion. To accommodate our limited time and space, without sacrificing the substance of the subject, we shall deal only with the mainstream theories that consist of the following:

*The Charles Darwin theory.*37 The famous author of the theory of evolution, Charles Darwin, posits the theory that emotions are essential to the evolution of the species because emotions allow and assist humans and animals to adapt to their environments in their struggle for survival.

The James-Lange theory. The psychologist William James and physiologist Carl Lange independently formulated the physiological theory of emotion that emotions are the effects of physiological reactions to physical stimulus.

The Schachter-Singer theory. This theory, which is also known as the two-factor theory of emotion, is the result of the collaboration of Stanley Schachter and his student Jerome Singer. Together, they came up with the theory that emotions are the effects of a two- stage process: first, the physiological response to stimulus and second, the experience of emotion.

The Cannon-Bard theory. This theory is also a result of the collaboration of two psychologists: Walter Cannon and Philip Bard. According to this theory, the physiological response to stimulus and the experience of emotion happen simultaneously and not as a result of a two-stage process as claimed by the Schachter-Singer theory.

The Lazarus theory. According to Richard Lazarus, emotion is produced according to the following sequence of events: first is the presence of stimulus, then followed by thought which recognized the stimulus, and subsequently, the simultaneous physiological and emotional responses to the stimulus. This is also known as the cognitive appraisal theory.

Important as these theories are in understanding emotion, to my mind, what is more important for us humans is in being able to deal properly with our emotion. To be able to do this, we should recognize the extremely important fact that we are *not* our emotion. Hence, we should understand that although our emotion is an integral part of our being, it does not define our being. Thus, our emotion and our being are two separate distinct entities. Hence, we should not identify with our emotion. We should not think that we are our emotion, that we and our emotion are *one*; otherwise, it would be impossible for us to deal with our emotion because as the saying goes, it takes *two* to tango, so to speak.

That is the first crucial step in dealing properly with our emotion: the recognition that we are *not* our emotion. The second crucial step is the recognition that the proper way to deal with our emotion is not to resist it but merely to observe it without making any judgment about it. The reason for this is the fact that the more you resist an emotion and the more you judge it as either positive or negative, the more it persists because the more you give energy to the emotion. Hence, so that an emotion will simply vanish for lack of energy, simply observe it as something apart from yourself, thereby cutting it off from its source of energy which is yourself. Having done this, you will be surprised how easy the whole natural process is, instead of agonizing in wanting it to disappear by resisting it.

This reminds me of the sad plight of the pitiful nuns and priests who made a vow of celibacy. This means that it is forbidden for them to engage in sexual activity. But as nature would have it, what is forbidden becomes more attractive. And so, these poor nuns and priests are relentlessly beset with the feeling of wanting to have sex, which they call lust. In their own words, they are always tempted to have sex, even solitary sex. But since they do not know the proper way how to deal with this natural feeling, they resort to the only way they know, which is to resist the feeling of wanting to have sex, to fight the temptation to have sex. In other words, there is always a war going on inside their being: a war between themselves and nature. But since one cannot fight nature and win, they always lose. This is the tragic plight of these poor ignorant nuns and priests.

The objective of the above discussion is to make us realize that despite the overwhelming power that an emotion can have on us, we are still in control and can make it disappear if we want to. Indeed, not only can we make an emotion disappear but also replace it with another emotion of our choice. For instance, if you feel sad and gloomy and you want to replace it with the positive feeling of joy, simply laugh or go through the motion of laughing and you will be surprised to find out that your motion or act of laughing will produce the emotion of joy or gaiety in you and at the same time replace your feeling of sadness.

There is a familiar song which exemplifies this emotional dynamic. It is called "I Whistle a Happy Tune." Its lyrics are as follows: "Whenever I feel afraid, I hold my head erect and whistle a happy tune, so no one will suspect I'm afraid. The result of this deception is very strange to tell, for when I fool the people, I feel I fool myself as well. I whistle a happy tune and every single time, the happiness in the tune convinces me that I'm not afraid."

The underlying reason why a change of behavior will result also in a change of emotion is the fact that we are really one substance. This means that the entire human system acts in a seamless holistic manner, so much so that even a slight pain in your forefinger will affect your entire being.

The importance to our happiness of the fact that we can create an emotion we prefer, just by performing the corresponding physical act even without any outside stimulus, cannot be overemphasized. This is all so true in our present stressful modern life where everything seems to be orchestrated to inflict to us emotional harm. In this negative environment harmful to our psyche, our only recourse to be happy and save our sanity is none other than ourselves. Thus, when we encounter hateful individuals, our natural tendency to nurse the feeling of hate, which will, of course, make us unhappy, should no longer be entertained. We can simply laugh, and voila, our unpleasant feeling of hatred will be replaced with the pleasant feeling of amusement and we are happy again. If we do this in any circumstance that will make us unhappy, then we will simply laugh all our problems off in our life.

This brings us to the importance of self-awareness. It is self-awareness which enables us to recognize the existence of the different emotions that we feel every moment of our life and, having recognized them, deal with them appropriately. Unless we have self- awareness, we will go through life half-awake or half-asleep; hence, not fully conscious of what is happening to us which prevents us from having full control of ourselves and our life resulting in the innumerable mistakes we do. This is the reason behind Christ's words uttered while he was hanging on the cross: "Father, forgive them for they do not know what they are doing." Indeed, how can we know what we are doing if we are only half-awake because we lack self-awareness?

This virtue of self-awareness or watchfulness is so important for Christ that he keeps on repeating it: "Watch, therefore, for you do not know what hour your Lord is coming" (Matthew 24:42). "Therefore you also be ready for the Son of Man is coming at an hour you do not expect" (Matthew 24:44). "Watch, therefore, for you know neither the day nor the hour when the Son of Man is coming" (Matthew 25:13).

Thus, the importance to our life of self-awareness—or watchfulness, in Christ's words—cannot be overemphasized. As long as people continue to believe in absurdities, so long will people continue to commit atrocities.

The underlying reason for this truth is the fact that self-awareness is the best way, if not the only way, to exercise control and mastery over ourselves and our life as humans. The other denizens of the animal kingdom cannot do this because they are governed by their instincts. Hence, it is by mastering our emotions that we are acting as truly humans. It is by mastering our emotions that we can ensure our happiness.

Chapter

12

Morality and Happiness

People are funny. They have classified almost everything into right and wrong or good and bad. Then they tell others to do what is right and avoid what is wrong, but they themselves do what is wrong and enjoy it. They also tell others to choose what is good and to reject what is bad, but they themselves choose what is bad and enjoy it. If this is not funny, it is utterly despicable. But I choose to call it funny or ludicrous (which comes from the Latin word "ludus," meaning game or play) since this life is a game anyway. And this is one of those games people love to play. Yes, people love to play this game called morality so much so that this game started even as early as the time of Adam and Eve in the garden of Eden. The biblical God classified the fruits of the garden into forbidden and not forbidden and then enjoined Adam to eat the latter but avoid the former on pain of sudden death. But since human nature is naturally attracted to what is forbidden, Adam ate the forbidden fruit, but he did not suddenly die. The biblical God simply drove him away from the garden of Eden. He still lived and begot three sons: Cain, Abel, and Seth and then died at the age of 930 years (Genesis 5:5). Even the biblical God loved to play this game of morality by telling a lie. Since then, this dangerous game became the human norm. Even the brilliant Aristotle himself joined this game. He wrote two books on ethics, a subject about morality, and named them after his sons. The followers of Aristotle in the academe also joined the game by making ethics an important component of the philosophy course. Or perhaps, as T. S. Eliot wisely observed: "Virtues are forced upon us by our impudent crimes."38 That is how pervasive morality's influence is on humans.

But why? Are there really right and wrong? Do good and bad really exist? Is morality then essential to human life and happiness? Or does it make human life more miserable? To be sure, existentially speaking, right and wrong do not exist. Neither good nor bad are realities. Human acts are simply human acts—no more, no less. So are things or objects, they are simply things or objects—no more, no less. But when judgmental people label a human act either right or wrong or an object either good or bad, they are simply making a moral judgment about the human act and the object in terms of how the human act or object affect them either positively or negatively. But their moral judgment does not in any way make the act or the object moral. The "right or wrong" or "good or bad" is not in the act or object but in their moral judgment. Hence, morality does not exist in reality but only in the mind of people making the moral judgment. People who are evil-minded or who are impure of heart see everything through dark moral glasses as evil. While people who are good-minded or pure of heart see everything through rosy moral glasses as good. A philosopher however wears no glasses and sees everything as simply everything. On the basis of my lengthy experience as an old man, it is absolutely clear to me that the unhappiest people on earth are the evil-minded ones. Ironically, they are usually those whose objective in life is to live a "good" life or a "holy" life. They see and hear evil wherever they go—even inside the church or in their own house or convent or monastery and especially inside their own head. And since they are trying their very best to live a holy or good life, they are tortured by what they see and hear and think, especially when it is about sex which they cannot resist because for them it is forbidden, and therefore extremely attractive. Nevertheless, they go through the futile process of resisting the sexual temptation. But the more they resist, the more the temptation persists. But since they are just humans, like Adam and Eve, they finally succumb to the temptation. Then, like Adam and Eve, they feel guilty and miserable. But only for a while. After asking God's forgiveness, they play the same miserable game all over again—all through their miserable life. Is this the way to live a happy life?

The pure of heart fare no better. If there is pure, there is also impure. If there is good, there is also bad. If the pure of heart see everything as good, they also see everything as bad because the good cannot exist without the bad and vice versa. Hence, there is a constant tug-of-war between the good and the bad in the mind of the pure of heart. If there is war, there is also misery. Hence, the pure of heart is also living a miserable life.

The philosopher, however, is made up of different stuff. The philosopher is not only like the proverbial monkey who sees and hears no evil, but also the philosopher thinks no evil. The fact is, the philosopher does not even think at all in the sense that he does not make moral judgment about reality one way or another. He simply accepts reality as it is. For the philosopher, there is nothing right or wrong, neither good nor bad. Everything simply is. His approach to reality is governed not by moral judgment but by the proper exercise of his free will. His choices depend solely on his will and not on the object of his choice since all objects are equally desirable as reality. Thus, he is not compelled even to make a choice. He can make or not make a choice. It all depends entirely on him. This is the state of true freedom. This is the state of nonattachment which spiritual pundits preach as essential to spiritual perfection. This is the real meaning of Christ's words: "Be in the world but not of the world."

Hence, only a philosopher lives truly as a man: a being with a free will. The rest of humanity are not really free. They are earthbound, marooned by their attachment to the world, confined within the illusory prison of their own mind.

Since freedom is essential to happiness, only philosophers, who are amoral and therefore not restrained by morality, are happy.

Hence, morality and happiness are like water and oil. They do not mix.

Nonthinking people do not realize that morality makes people more immoral. Why? Because morality is based on the principle that people should do good and avoid evil. In other words, morality, in essence, is a rule limiting human conduct. But humans are essentially free. Freedom is an essential quality of being human. Since this is so, anything that restricts human freedom is abhorrent to human nature. And therefore, the tendency of human nature vis- à-vis restriction or prohibition is to fight it. This is the reason why humans have the tendency to violate rules and regulations since rules and regulations, in essence, restrict and limit human freedom. That is why we have a dictum which says that rules are meant to be broken. That is why what is prohibited is attractive in the sense that humans are compelled to violate it.

Now, morality, as previously said, is a restriction and limitation to human freedom. Therefore, the tendency of free humans is to violate morality by breaking its rules, if only to assert or exercise their freedom. No wonder, for humans, what is prohibited becomes more attractive because it attracts the natural tendency of humans to violate it.39 Hence, in this sense, morality makes humans more immoral. Instead of making people good, morality does the opposite. Now, since morality makes humans more immoral, morality is counterproductive. Instead of making humans do its bidding,
morality makes humans do the opposite, as previously stated.

No wonder, religious people who made the vow to be moral are actually immoral. It is not really their fault. They are simply compelled by their human nature to violate the rules of morality that actually violate their freedom. In existential terms, morality is a violation of human nature and when humans violate morality, it is human nature's way of simply fighting back and giving morality a taste of its own medicine, so to speak. Hence, one cannot fight nature with impunity. One cannot fight nature and win. That is why religion is losing the war on morality.

The best way to make humans, especially children, do what you want them to do is to appeal to their reason by showing them that what you want them to do is really for their well-being because it will redound to their own benefit, to their own happiness. This type of persuasion is so effective because it is in harmony not only with the rational nature of humans but also with their God-given freedom.40 It is not only effective, but more importantly, it redounds to human happiness.

In sum, morality has nothing to do with happiness, but everything to do with misery since it is a violation of human nature.

Chapter

13

Money and Happiness

Money is everything!" That is the favorite mantra of people today. Living in this so-called modern world where everything costs money, that kind of attitude is perfectly normal and understandable. Nowadays, even love costs money—and more so. No matter how good-looking you are but you have no money, you would be absolutely lucky if you can find somebody who will really love you. But no matter how old and ugly you are, if you live in a big house, drive a BMW or a Mercedes, can afford to dine regularly in expensive restaurants, and most importantly, have a solid income, then you are made. You will have no problem about your love life. When your pocket is ready, your love will appear. That is the current law on love and money.

That is the picture of life nowadays regarding money. At first glance, it looks nice and pretty. But at further scrutiny, it is really ugly. Not only ugly but terrifying as well. For most people, in order to have a good life, they have to spend all their precious life making money. They have to live like a workhorse so they can have all the things they think will make them happy so they can enjoy life. But when they are finally able to achieve this goal, they are too old or too sick or both to enjoy the things that money can buy and therefore can no longer enjoy life. They find themselves in a nursing home. And perhaps, during one of those starlit nights, they look at the starry sky through the small window they share with their similarly situated roommates and wonder what went wrong, what happened to their dream of happiness. Or in a worst-case scenario, they are not even able to ask those questions because they are suffering from Alzheimer's. And so, they just stare at the starry sky with mindless eyes. It is indeed a sad scenario. But sadly to say, it is a common one, especially here in the land of American dream. It is a tragic scenario created no doubt by the omnipotent director called money. Is there no way to change this ugly script? Is there no light at the end of this dark monetary tunnel of life?

There are several important principles about money that people in general are not aware of. Hence, they unknowingly violate these principles resulting in the tragic situation pictured above. The first and foremost is money cannot buy happiness. To be sure, money can buy some of the essential ingredients of happiness like food, clothing, and shelter, but it cannot buy happiness itself. This is so because, as previously discussed, happiness is an intangible satisfaction or fulfillment of human needs resulting in intangible pleasure as a natural reward for the satisfaction of these natural needs. Moreover, you may be able to buy some of the things that your body and mind require for their needs, but you cannot buy all of them. For instance, you cannot buy rest and exercise that your body needs for its health. You simply have to take the trouble of going to sleep and performing exercises. Similarly with the mind. You may be able to buy books for your mind to acquire knowledge, but you have to read those books and think about what you read in order to satisfy your mind's needs for knowledge. And more so with your spirit. There is practically nothing you can buy to satisfy your spirit. You have to perform what your spirit requires for its needs. Hence, money is not all that omnipotent when it comes to happiness. But a lot of people are either unaware of this or disregard it completely.

Indeed, people think they can get away with anything by means of money. A lot of people who go to church and put several hundreds of dollars in the collection box do so thinking that God will return the favor by forgiving their sins, answering their prayers, and giving them more money. They think they can buy even God. This kind of shocking, erroneous mentality is extremely dangerous. It is not only a shocking insult to God but even gives the doer the wrong motivation to commit more sins since forgiveness can be bought anyway. This is another cause of recidivism. No wonder crimes continue unabated. This is also the cause of the bloody Protestant Reformation initiated by the famous German Augustinian friar, Martin Luther, in protest against the corrupt practice by the Catholic Church of selling indulgences for the remission of sins.

Another essential feature of money that eludes a lot of people is that there is enough money for the satisfaction of human needs, but not enough money for the satisfaction of human wants. Why so? Because human needs are few and limited, whereas human wants are numerous and unlimited. Hence, no matter what you do, you cannot have enough money to satisfy all your wants. Hence, if you think that happiness consists in producing enough money to satisfy all your wants, think again. That kind of thinking is the sure formula for failure and unhappiness in life. This is clearly shown by the tragic lives of people who have seemingly achieved financial success but, at the end of the day, commit suicide.

Human wants, to repeat, can never be satisfied because they are infinite. Hence, no amount of money can satisfy them. This is why happiness is limited only to the satisfaction of human needs but not to human wants. Human wants are a bunch of monsters that keep on multiplying and growing the more you feed them until you can no longer feed them and they eventually feed on you. If there is a lesson you have to learn early in life for your success and happiness, this is it. It is part of wisdom not to try to achieve what is impossible. But note well that the "want" we are referring to is the "want for material things" that people think can give them happiness. Want for the spiritual things in life is another thing. It is absolutely laudable and much to be desired and developed as an essential part of one's evolution for endless perfection. But then, ironically, this is the kind of want that people do not have. Their focus in life is to satisfy their want for a more expensive car, for a bigger and more beautiful house, for more and more money, and so on ad infinitum until they die of diseases caused by working hard to make more and more money to satisfy their monstrous want for material things. This is the tragic life of humans.

Another important principle about money is that it is a human tool to facilitate the exchange of goods and services among humans. I am sure you know this only too well. Money, indeed, is an efficient tool for this purpose. However, it is so efficient that it morphed into a monster that it is today. Money has become an effective means of buying power, fame, loyalty, politicians, police, sex, love, etc. Name it and money can buy it—except, of course, happiness, although some people think otherwise. Thus, money has become so powerful that people, instead of being the masters of money, have become its slaves. Instead of using money, people are being used by money. That is the tragedy resulting from losing the proper perspective about money. It is a tragedy that is wrecking havoc on the precious lives of people. This is the meaning of the dictum that love of money is the root of all evils. Note well that it is not money that is the root of all evils. But love of money is.[41]

Perhaps, it is time to abolish money. But that is hardly the solution. The solution is to abolish the wrong attitude about money; that it is necessary for human happiness. People should realize that nothing can be further from the truth. People should be grounded in the truth that happiness is found inside man and *not* outside man— those things that money can buy. People should realize the real meaning of Christ's words: "The kingdom of God is within you."

In sum, money is not essential for human happiness. An erroneous view about money will inevitably cause the human sufferings that bedevil human life. But money, seen with the right perspective and thus used properly, can enhance human happiness and be used as an effective tool for good and can hasten the coming of peace to our troubled weary world.

Chapter

14

Drugs and Happiness

Once upon a turbulent time in human history, Karl Marx, an outstanding Russian philosopher, bravely and wisely gave to the whole world a piece of wisdom encapsulated in these famous words: "Religion is the opium of the masses." The truth of Karl Marx's observation gives more weight and veracity to our thesis in chapter 11 of this book that religion is the devil in disguise, that like a drug, it gives a false sense of happiness to its numerous victims. Hence, in this chapter, "Drug and Happiness," we will take a cue from Karl Marx and define *drug* as anything which humans use as a false substitute for happiness, like religion.

The unabated proliferation and use of different kinds of drugs by humans nowadays are symptomatic of their failure to find happiness. Since real happiness is hard to come by, the natural demand for happiness compels people to find a substitute, and according to Karl Marx, religion has become that much needed substitute. But has it really? To be sure, the proliferation of different kinds of religion has reached such a proportion that religion can indeed be called a drug. However, aside from religion, people keep on using different kinds of drugs without letup and the problems it creates keep on increasing daily. Hence, it seems that this latter phenomenon belies Karl Marx's assessment. Indeed, this is a social conundrum, a baffling social phenomenon. If Karl Marx were correct, then religion should be able to trump drugs. But the facts show otherwise: religion and drugs are the two major problems of the world today. So it seems that religion is not that effective after all. It seems that it is losing its tight hold on people's consciousness that has become used to religion's shopworn teachings and machinations. But still, religion has not fully lost its deadly sting. A particular brand of religion has completely dominated the consciousness of some people that it is creating such violence in the world that it is now the primary current problem in the world. I am sure you know what I mean.

Anyway, if during the time of Marx, religion is the opium of the masses, today, drug is the religion of the people. The poor and the rich, the illiterate and the educated, the young and the old, nay, people from all walks of life pay homage to and worship drugs. And like religion, drugs are legion and have different brands and names. Indeed, there are many parallelisms between drugs and religion. This is because of the fact that people in their futile search for happiness have turned to these inventions of society as substitute for the real thing. But as expected, they are poor substitutes. They are not only poor substitutes but harmful substitutes. These are shown by recent tragic events concerning pedophile priests whose precious lives are ruined by religion. These are shown by recent tragic events concerning Hollywood celebrities whose precious lives were untimely extinguished by drugs. We know these facts through the media. But what about those cases that are not worthy of media's attention? What about those unknown cases involving unknown people whose equally precious lives are equally victims of religion and drugs? Who are they and how many are they? We will never know and need not know. All we need to know is that they are as important and significant as those publicized by the media. All we need to know is that they are also people like you and me who have inalienable rights to the pursuit of happiness but never found it because they were lured by the false promises of religion and drugs. Yes, we will never know and need not know their mental grief and the spiritual despair of their hapless lives spent in futile suffering. All we know and need to know is the tragic fact that there are indeed these miserable events in human life involving real people, events that have become so ordinary and commonplace that they are no longer newsworthy even in an insignificant corner of a cheap tabloid. Yet in a deeper and more meaningful level, these insignificant events are not really that insignificant. They bespeak of the unspeakable longing of an immortal soul for the transcendental necessity of his being: happiness. It is a longing beyond time and space, a longing that tears apart the fabric of eternity and demands for the imperative goal of human existence: happiness. And yet it is a goal that is not really difficult to achieve because happiness is always there, always with us—if only we know how to find it.

It is my fervent wish and undying hope that this book will show the correct path to that elusive human goal of happiness which will eventually realize humanity's universal dream of peace on earth.

Chapter

15

Laughter and Happiness

Laughter is the best medicine" is a worn-out dictum. Why it became such speaks volumes of the long ongoing history of the human experience of its veracity. Indeed, laughter is truly a good, if not the best, medicine. Why this is so is not really obvious. What is obvious is the fact that laughter makes us feel good. Why this is so is also not obvious. It simply makes us feel good. Period. We do not really care why. What we truly care about is the fact that it makes us feel good. And that alone is a big deal. In this life, where there are many reasons why we should feel bad, feeling good is truly a big deal, especially if it costs us nothing as laughter does. And even if we have to pay for it, we really do not mind as long as we are able to laugh and feel good in the process. This is the reason for the popularity of comedians we have to pay just to make us laugh. This is the reason why we love funny movies and stand-up comedies.

But why does laughter have such a reputation as a good medicine? Does feeling good have a medicinal value? If so, why? The answer may be found in the case of my friend who was sick of cancer. My friend, however, did not want to avail of the standard medical cure of chemotherapy or radiation therapy because the people he knows who underwent these therapies not only lost their precious hair but also their hard-earned money and never gained back their precious health and eventually lost their precious life. Despite of, or perhaps because of, his refusal to be a victim of chemotherapy and radiation therapy, he is now a healthy person fully cured of his cancer. A miracle? Not really. My friend, knowing that his cancer was caused by his stressful life and therefore stress is the real cause of his deadly disease, put two and two together and decided to undergo an unorthodox therapy, consisting of getting rid of the cause (stress) of his disease. How? Every day for one solid hour, he did nothing but laugh. Surprise! After a month of laughing, his cancer started to slowly disappear till finally he achieved complete remission. Does my friend's unique case prove that feeling good has a medicinal value? Is laughter the cause of the remission of my friend's cancer?

Medical science with its stringent requirements for proof will answer, of course, in the negative. My friend, however, who is now living a happy, cancer-free life, will thumb his nose and even give a finger at medical science and will absolutely answer in the positive. Who is right, medical science or my friend?

If laughter is really the cause of the cure of my friend's cancer— and I totally agree with him—what is the reason behind this amazing power of laughter that it has trumped medical science, which, up to now, despite its vaunted modern healing supremacy, has not really found an effective cure for cancer? The answer may be found in the nature and dynamics of laughter and its intimate relationship with happiness.

In layman's language, laughter is nothing more than the sound we produce when we laugh. But why do we laugh, and what happens when we laugh? From experience, we know that there are really many reasons why we laugh. We laugh when we feel joy. We laugh when we are tickled. We laugh when we are amused and the reasons why we are amused are legion. Hence, the reasons why we laugh are innumerable. The ultimate reason for this is the human mind. The human mind is so potent that it can see numberless reasons for laughter. Thus, it takes intelligence to be able to laugh. No wonder of all the numberless species in the animal kingdom, only the intelligent human species has the ability to really laugh.

But what happens to us when we laugh? Laugh and see what happens to you when you laugh. Not only do you feel good but also your internal organs also feel good. When you feel good, you are relieved of your stresses and you feel relaxed. When your internal organs feel good, that happens because the physical action of laughing produces motions in your body that give your internal organs the exercise they need for their health. Hence, a person who laughs a lot is normally a healthy person. And since health is essential for happiness, a person who laughs a lot is a happy person.

That, in simple layman's language, is the dynamics of laughter and its intimate relationship with happiness.

Stress, to be sure, is not completely bad. Normal stress is also good for the health of humans. It also serves as instrument for the human system to achieve its need to relax since stress and relaxation go together as day and night. To be able to relax and fall asleep (the ultimate relaxation) during the night, one has to be active and absorb normal stress during the day. But abnormal stress is altogether a different thing. It is bad for the human health. Stress becomes abnormal when one absorbs too much stress that prevents him from falling asleep and thus makes him unable to achieve the ultimate relaxation which should enable him to absorb more stress during the day. The reason why this unfortunate event happens can be traced to the human nervous system and the very stressful modern life of humans.

Humans have a nervous system which can absorb only a limited amount of stress, much like an electric bulb which is designed to absorb only a limited amount of electricity. When an electric bulb exceeds the amount of electricity it absorbs, it bursts. Similarly, when the human nervous system exceeds the amount of stress it absorbs because of the very stressful life humans live, then the human nervous system is injured and disabled, resulting in an impaired human being.

To prevent this disaster from happening to yourself, it is essential that you should be aware of the crucial relationship between yourself and the stressful modern life you are living. Each person has his own unique capacity for absorbing stress; hence, you should be aware of your own unique capacity to handle stress. Make sure your system receives only the amount of stress it can handle. To do this, you should make use of laughter to assist your nervous system. Hence, you should laugh a lot during the day. The beauty of laughter is that it is under your control. You can laugh even without a reason to laugh. How? Just laugh. Go through the motion of laughing. If you do that, you will find out to your surprise that you are really laughing not for any funny reason but simply because you want to laugh. By doing this, you will also find out that you can control your emotion, and thus, you become master of yourself. And the best time to do this is when you feel down or when you are angry or when you feel anything that gives you stress.

Laugh and the world will laugh with you.

Chapter

16

Sorrow and Happiness

God is absolute and God exists in an absolute world. Do you understand this? If you don't, neither do I. It is really extremely difficult to think about God, let alone write about this unknown being whose nature is absolutely beyond our understanding and comprehension. This is because we live in a relative world where everything is understood only in terms of its opposite. Thus, we have night and day, up and down, good and bad, etc. Notice that we understand "night" only with reference to "day," "up" to "down," "good" to "bad," and vice versa. This fact is so obvious and commonplace that it escapes our attention. We even do not think about it. We do not think that there can be no day without night, no white without black, no good without bad, no beautiful without ugly, no joy without pain. And yet this is a given fact of our relative existence, a fact which we cannot escape as long as we live in this relative world.

The funny thing about us humans, or the irony of our existence, is that we do not really understand and appreciate our relative existence. We do not understand and appreciate why we live in a world of opposites, a world of positive and negative, a world of what the Chinese call the yang and the yin, the male and female principles of life. Take the reality of "good" and "evil," for instance. We want everything to be good so much so that we cannot reconcile ourselves to the things we call evil—like pain, disease, suffering, and everything we loathe, hate, and despise. We keep on asking why God created evil. We keep on repeating the mantra that if God is truly good, why does he allow evil to exist, and if he truly loves us, why does he allow us to suffer. These stupid questions simply show that we humans are not at home in the world we live in. We long for a different world, a world of eternal summer and eternal sunshine. We heave a sigh of relief when the harsh winter is finally over and spring, the harbinger of summer, has finally come. We are like the poet Shelley who wrote this immortal line at the end of his beautiful poem, "Ode to the West Wind": "If Winter comes can Spring be far behind?" And we want all our wishes to come true. We are so unhappy when we are disappointed. We cannot stand pain. We want our roses without thorns.

This kind of unrealistic attitude about the realities of life makes us total strangers in this world of opposites—unhappy strangers. Unless we feel at home in this world, the only world we know, we cannot be truly happy. We will always be living in what Shakespeare calls "the winter of discontent." It is therefore an imperative task that in this book about happiness, we address properly this issue which is visceral to human happiness so that we will have spring even when it is winter.

The law of opposites is the supreme inevitable transcendental universal law. Hence, it applies even to God. This is the reason why God created the relative world, the world of opposites. God has to create the relative world in consonance with this law. Why? Because without the relative world, God would not be able to understand and appreciate his own absolute world because there is nothing to compare it with. Hence, even his own absolute being is meaningless without the relative. Now, since God is everything, it follows that the worlds of the absolute and the relative, which compose the totality of everything, coexist in God's being. Thus, God is both absolute and relative, both one and many. Contradiction? Maybe so. But such is reality. It is made up of contradictions. And God is the supreme contradiction.

In light of that simplified metaphysics and cosmology in capsule form, the mystery of evil is no longer a mystery, contrary to the perception of religious people. It is perfectly understandable. Evil is a necessity. It is necessary so that we can understand and appreciate its opposite: the good. Good is meaningless without evil. If everything is good, good does not exist because there is nothing to compare or contrast it with. Hence, good, like God, cannot exist alone. It needs evil to exist.

Sorrow is similarly situated. For a lot of people, sorrow is evil. But life without sorrow is meaningless. And a life without meaning does not exist. Sorrow, therefore, is an essential ingredient of life. It makes life more exciting. It makes life more joyful. It makes life more meaningful and challenging. That is why the poet Shelley wrote: "Our sweetest songs are those that tell of saddest thoughts." In the beautiful painting of life, sorrow stands for the dark hues that complement and highlight the bright colors of existence. In the great symphony of life, sorrow expresses dramatically those sweet sounds of the violins that moderate and complement the deafening clash of cymbals.

Hunger is similarly situated. Most people abhor hunger. For them, hunger is evil. When they are hungry, they are so miserable until they are full. But how do they know they are full without the experience of hunger? How do they know and appreciate the blissful feeling of being full without experiencing hunger pangs? This reminds me of an episode in my life when I became a guest of a family, a very rich family who had to celebrate for one week several important family events. For one solid week, they celebrated with food, food, and more food. Hence, for one solid week, there was nothing to do but eat, eat, and eat. For one solid week, I had to eat even when I was not hungry. For one solid week, I forgot the feeling of being hungry. Before the week ended, I no longer enjoyed eating. Eating became a pure punishment. Hence, I learned from that personal experience the all-important lesson that without hunger pangs, there can be no pleasure of being full. Since then, so that I will enjoy eating, I wait for my hunger pangs to come.

This is the supreme reason why we live in a relative world, a world of constant change, change from one opposite to another so that we can enjoy life and be happy. This is the reason why we have four seasons.

Otherwise, summer will no longer be summer. Hence, contrary to the perception of others, we live in a perfect world where not only good but also evil exist. Evil, therefore, is not the mystery religion teaches. It is a rational and existential necessity. Evil is necessary for us humans to understand and appreciate the necessary good. Evil complements good. The devil complements God. This is the real answer to the problem of evil which eludes the religious people. It is not a problem after all, but a blessing in disguise. (This is discussed more extensively in the next chapter.)

Similarly, sorrow complements happiness. Do not therefore hate sorrow because sorrow makes you understand and appreciate happiness better. Your smile is sweeter after you have shed tears. Your laughter is more joyful after you cry. Your joy is more blissful after an agony of pain.

Life is more beautiful because of death and peace is more cherished because of war.

Chapter

17

Evil and Happiness

The problem of evil is the number one problem which haunts religion, especially the Catholic religion. Why? Because it is a problem to which religion has no adequate answer, that is why. And yet it is the number one problem that followers of religion are desperately asking for solution. And the so-called all-knowing priests who are being asked for adequate answers by their followers can only come up with the pitiful answer: mystery. Yes, the existence of evil in this world is simply a mystery. That is the pitiful answer of these all-knowing priests to the problem of evil. Of course, it goes without saying that such a pitiful answer is simply unsatisfactory to humans who are tortured by numerous sufferings which they perceive as evil. The answer is not only unsatisfactory but spawns more problems.

Another unsatisfactory answer to the problem of evil is found in the story of Job in the Bible. According to the Bible, Job is a righteous man who was tested by God at the prodding of the devil. The test consists of giving Job so much suffering to find out if he can still be righteous despite all his sufferings. Job passed the test with flying colors. But according to religion, that is not the point of the story. The moral lesson is that the evils of this world that make humans suffer are just tests given by God to find out if despite all these evils, humans can still be righteous and therefore faithful to God. That is the moral lesson of the fictitious story of Job, according to religion. Hence, when followers of religion ask their priests about the problem of evil, this is also another answer given to them: like Job, they are also being tested by God. But when pressed why God should test them, these all-knowing priests will again give the same answer: mystery. Indeed, why should God test Job and other humans? If God is truly all-knowing, does he not know whether Job or any person will pass his test or not? If he does, what is the point of giving the test? Is that not an insult to the all-knowing God who should know whether someone can pass the test or not? Truly, the fact that these so-called all-knowing priests keep on saying that God is merely testing people by giving them problems in their lives, this fact alone speaks volumes of their abysmal ignorance. They do not even realize that they are actually insulting God.

Indeed, when these priests do not know the real answer to any problem of life, their typical classic answer is mystery. Is mystery, therefore, the real answer to the problem of evil? Is it the sad destiny of humans to suffer in ignorance all their life about this supreme problem of life called evil?

The answer to these demanding questions necessitates a satisfactory answer. Hence, although this issue has already been slightly dealt with in the previous chapter, the author seriously feels that in fairness to the reader, a better answer should be given. Hence, this chapter.

As a matter of fact, the problem of evil has really nothing to do with religion. That is the reason why religious advocates have no satisfactory answer to it. That is the reason why priests cannot really answer it. The problem really belongs to the realm of philosophy. And philosophy says that existentially speaking, no such problem exists. Where then is the problem? The problem exists only in the mind of religious people who do not understand evil and therefore erroneously think that evil exists but cannot satisfactorily account for it. Evil, therefore, is simply a mental fiction. It is not real. Let me explain.

For a better understanding of evil, we have to define it. According to the lexicon, evil is "the fact of suffering, misfortune, and wrongdoing; something that brings sorrow, distress, or calamity." Everybody can agree with this definition of evil. Hence, it is an excellent definition of evil. However, take note that "suffering, misfortune, wrongdoing, sorrow, distress, and calamity" do not exist in reality. They are, like evil, the result of mental judgment of people regarding facts or realities that happen in their lives that they perceived to be negative or undesirable. Hence, they are, like evil, simply mental constructs. They are not real. Again, let me explain.

For instance, if a person gets bankrupt and because of his bankruptcy he suffers, it is normal for that person to think that his bankruptcy is evil. And so is his suffering. But a philosophical analysis of the situation tells us that neither his bankruptcy nor his suffering is evil. For instance, if the enemy of that person learns of the latter's bankruptcy and suffering, that enemy will normally be happy and think that it is good for that person to be bankrupt and suffer. And so, who is right, that bankrupt person or his enemy? The answer is neither of them is correct. Bankruptcy and suffering are neither good nor evil. The good and evil exist not in reality but only in the mind of those who think of reality as such. If that bankrupt person is able to find a way to deliver himself from his bankruptcy and becomes richer than before, obviously this is good for that person but evil or bad for his enemy. Again, neither of them is right or wrong. The evil or good is only in their judgmental minds.

Therefore, evil does not exist. Since evil does not exist, there is no such thing as a problem of evil. It also exists only in the minds of people.

Indeed, evil does not really exist. Hence, the question why God created evil or allowed evil to exist in this world is a misplaced question. Actually, such a stupid question is a terrible insult to God. It means that God is not really almighty and all-powerful so that his creation is not perfect but questionable.

Moreover, granted for the sake of argument, that evil exists, the existence of evil is a necessary given in the relative scheme of things in this relative world where we live, as previously discussed. Evil has to exist in order to complement good. If there is no evil and everything is good, then good does not exist because there is nothing to compare or contrast it with. Hence, evil has to exist in order for good to exist. That in simple terms is the reality of relative life. As the French say, "C'est la vie."

Furthermore, if looked upon in the light of evolution, which is the reason for our existence, evil is good. Why? Because evolution in practical terms is simply the successful struggle of living things to adapt to the negative influences in their environment. This successful struggle enables living things to develop superior characteristics in order not only to survive but also to progress to a superior state of life.42 These negative influences are what is pejoratively called evil. Seen in this perspective, therefore, evil is not only good but even necessary for the evolution of living things, including humans.

Indeed, evil is not only good but necessary for human evolution. In terms of medicine, for example, evil stands for the foreign bodies in the human system. Because of these foreign bodies, that the human immune system has to fight in order for the human system to remain healthy and survive, the human immune system becomes strong. Now, in layman's language, these foreign bodies are also pejoratively called dirt which people call bad or evil without realizing that this evil dirt is necessary for their health. This is simply the principle behind the medical practice called vaccination which enables humans to remain healthy despite the onset of disease because vaccination makes their immune system strong. No wonder people who hate dirt and are so clean have weak immune systems and are, therefore, sickly.

In sum, evil is not only good but necessary for humans to survive and evolve.

So much then for the so-called test or problem or mystery called evil.

To highlight the futility of and how ludicrous this so-called problem of evil is, let me share with you the story about a farmer and his ubiquitous neighbors. One day, the farmer found out that his horse he uses for plowing his field has run away. When his neighbors knew about this, they went to the farmer right away and told him how sorry they were for the bad thing that happened to him. The farmer, however, simply shrugged his shoulders and said to them,

"Who knows what is good or what is bad?" After a few days, the farmer's horse returned with other horses it befriended. When his neighbors knew about this, they again went to the farmer and told him how happy they were for his good fortune. Again, the farmer simply shrugged his shoulders and muttered, "Who knows what is good or what is bad?" After a few days, the farmer's son has to be taken to the hospital after he fell down from one of the wild horses. When his neighbors knew about this, they again went to the farmer to express their sorrow for the bad fortune of his son. Again, the farmer simply shrugged his shoulder and murmured, "Who knows what is good or what is bad?" After several weeks, the farmer's son returned fully healed and brought with him as his bride the beautiful lady doctor who took care of him in the hospital. The news quickly travelled to the farmer's neighbors who quickly expressed their joy to the farmer and his son for their good fortune. Again, the farmer uttered his favorite mantra: "Who knows what is good or what is bad?" This time, draw your own conclusion.

Chapter

18

Salvation and Happiness

Humans suffer from a psychological disease which I call the salvation complex. The most obvious symptom of this disease is the existence of countless churches or places of worship of countless religions all over the world offering salvation for their countless members. Another symptom is the religious doctrines of sin, heaven, and hell as the reasons for the salvation being offered. On the business side, another symptom is the lucrative insurance business to save people from poverty when they are old.

The entire complex structure of religion is built on this delusion called salvation. Salvation from what? Salvation from eternal damnation in hellish punishment. The monstrosity and irrationality of this extreme and irrational punishment is enough to show the deceptive and false nature of this monstrous idea, which only a sick and deluded mind can conceive. Nonetheless, for the sake of argument, let us unravel this colossal madness and expose its true distorted irrational nature.

There are two versions of this doctrine called salvation: the Catholic version and the Muslim version. The Catholic version says that when a person dies with an unforgiven mortal sin in his soul, even if it is the first mortal sin he committed in his entire life, he simply goes to hell to suffer for all eternity. Again, the utter atrocity of this idea is enough to destroy its credibility, let alone its veracity. The Muslim version is basically the same but with an additional dramatic effect. It says that if an infidel or an enemy of Allah dies, he goes to eternal hell where his body will be used as fuel for the fires of hell.43 Truly, imaginative idea, indeed! However, the two versions share the following identical features: First, it is utterly a brazen contradiction of the doctrine of an all-merciful God found in the teachings of both religions. Second, as an obvious corollary of the first, it is a shocking insult to God's supreme intelligence and infinite goodness. Third, it is a simplistic but clever manipulation of the human basic instinct for survival in order to control the weak minds of humans. Let us parse these issues.

First: Hell vs. the All-Merciful God

Religion teaches that hell is a punishment by God for man's sin. To understand fully this egregious insanity, we have to understand fully the entire history and concept of sin in terms of the Catholic teaching on the matter. The Church teaches the beautiful, although baseless, doctrine that God so loves the world that he sends his only begotten Son [Jesus Christ] to save the world. This is the doctrine of redemption, which is one of the major pillars of the fictional edifice that the Church really is. It is based on the erroneous reading but clever interpretation of the story of Adam and Eve in the Bible. This issue has been thoroughly discussed in my other book entitled *God's Advocate*. However, we have to mention it here to elucidate the issue of sin and redemption. The Church teaches that because Adam and Eve disobeyed God by eating the so-called forbidden fruit, they committed the first sin, the so-called original sin. And the effects of the original sin are the following: First, God drove Adam and Eve from the Garden of Eden. Second, Adam and Eve lost the gift of immortality. Third, the gates of heaven were closed to Adam and Eve and to the rest of mankind who inherited the original sin of their first parents. Fourth, in order to reopen the gates of heaven, God sent his only begotten son to redeem man by dying on the cross. Fifth, original sin gave human nature a flaw which made humans susceptible to sin. Let us again parse these beautiful teachings.

The first and second effects were discussed and refuted in my other book, *God's Advocate*. The third, fourth, and fifth effects are simply products of the wild imagination of the Church. They have no factual basis whatsoever nor scriptural justification whatsoever. They are mere fictitious doctrines of the Church that their followers have to take by faith. They are mere concoctions of the Church in order to control the minds of people and have power over them. I need not prove these statements. They are blatantly obvious to intelligent and unbiased observers. The real proof is the scandalous history of the Church from the past to the present.

Let me now expound a bit more on the issue of sin which is symptomatic of the human salvation complex. Sin is the hottest issue on earth. Everybody talks about sin. I still have to meet somebody like me who does not buy this religious commodity called sin. So you also think there is really sin? Think again. What is sin, really? The Church defines sin as a violation of the will of God. This definition is based on the assumption that the will of God can be violated. So you really think the will of God can be violated? Think again! What happened to the religious doctrine that God is omnipotent, all-powerful? Will such an almighty and all-knowing being allow his will to be violated? Also, what happened to the Church doctrine that everything happens in accordance with the will of God? If this is so, how can there be violation of the will of God? Granting that there can be violation of the will of God, that violation will also be in accordance with the will of God since everything happens in accordance with the divine will. Hence, in the final analysis, there can really be no violation of the will of God. To violate God's will is an absolute impossibility. Hence, the statement, "Violation of the will of God," is an unadulterated oxymoron. Hence, sin as a violation of the will of God does not and cannot exist. Is the logic crystal clear?

To go to the extent of beating a dead horse, so to speak, I shall put the above argument in a syllogistic form: What is not in accordance with the will of God does not exist. But sin is not in accordance with the will of God. Therefore, sin does not exist. This is a perfect syllogism just like the classic syllogism: All men are mortal. You are a man. Therefore, you are mortal. The major premise (what is not in accordance with the will of God does not exist) is simply the double negative version of the teaching of the Church that everything exists in accordance with the will of God. There should be no dispute on this matter which is a universal truth and acceptable to anyone who believes in God. But of course, if you do not believe in God, if you do not subscribe to the existence of God, this argument does not apply to you.

The minor premise (sin is not in accordance with the will of God) is simply the Church's definition of sin which is a violation of the will of God and therefore not in accordance with the divine will.

The conclusion (sin does not exist) flows logically and inexorably from the major and minor premises.

For the reader who did not study logic or was absent when the class is discussing syllogism, syllogism is simply a reasoning process based on the obvious principle that two things that are equal to the same thing are also equal to one another. In mathematical form: 1=3, 2=3, 1=2. In our syllogism, (1) "sin" and (2) "does not exist" are both (3) "what is not in accordance with the will of God." Therefore, (1) "sin" (2) "does not exist."

If you studied Aristotelian logic, the above explanation should be crystal clear to you. But if you did not, my crystal clear explanation should produce the same effect.

Anyway (this is really beating a dead horse), the bottom line of all these exercises is the fact that there is no sin. Sin does not exist and there is no valid proof for the existence of sin. If you want to put it another way, either there is God whose divine omnipotence created everything in accordance with his omnipotent will, or there is sin which is a violation of that will and therefore not in accordance with it. But there is God. Therefore, there is no sin. In other words, the idea of an omnipotent God who created everything in accordance with his will trumps the idea of the existence of sin. Hence, God and sin cannot coexist. Either you choose God or you choose sin. You cannot have both because they are logically incompatible. If you do, you will be contradicting yourself. You will be guilty of an oxymoron. And you will be a moron.

But what about the objection that God gave humans free will, and therefore, humans can violate God's will and thus commit sin? Is not that a valid argument against our thesis that God's will cannot be violated, and therefore, there can be no sin? That is exactly the argument of the Church which we shall shortly demolish and make a short shrift of and even show that it actually proves our thesis instead of demolishing it. The simple logic of the matter is simply this: Since it is God himself who gave humans free will (a fact which nobody disputes, much less by the Church since this is exactly what the Church teaches), it follows that whatever humans do with their free will should also be in accordance with the will of God. Therefore, humans cannot violate the will of God by their exercise of their free will which is a gift of God. Perhaps a simple analogy might clarify the matter. If I give you a blank check, it is understood that I will honor whatever amount you will write in that blank check. Therefore, I have no reason to complain if you will write the huge amount of one billion in that blank check. Similarly, since God gave you a free will, it is understood that you can do anything in the exercise of that free will since it is free and thus has no restriction. Therefore, God cannot be offended by anything you will do in the exercise of your free will since it is free, and God gave it to you, knowing that it is free. Therefore, whatever you do is in accordance with the will of God and has God's blessing. In such a situation, how can you offend God in the exercise of your free will? Therefore, the argument regarding free will does not in any way diminish our thesis. On the contrary, it just affirms it.

Let us expound further the fact that our free will is a gift from God, and therefore, we cannot offend God by the exercise of our free will. A gift is a gift. In legal parlance, a gift is an unconditional donation by a donor to a donee. Since the donation is unconditional (no strings attached), the donee can do anything about the donation (the gift) without violating the will of the donor. So also, in the case of our free will, since it is an unconditional donation (a gift) by God (the donor) to us humans (the donees), we can do anything about our free will without violating God's will. In other words, God has made our will his own. Thus, whatever we do in the exercise of our will is in accordance with God's own will. In short, humans cannot violate the will of God in any way.

The logic of the matter is simplicity itself and indisputable. And yet the all-knowing Catholic Church is absolutely befuddled about this issue of free will in connection with sin. The omniscient Church has even a wrong concept of what free will is all about. The Church defines free will as the ability to do what is right but not what is wrong. In other words, the Church is giving restriction or limitation to the idea of freedom, which is obviously a contradiction. If freedom has limitation or restriction, how can it be freedom? Does not the all-wise Church know that the concept of freedom and the concept of limitation or restriction negate each other? Is the Church so ignorant not to know that "conditional freedom" is an oxymoron? To be candid, I am really sick and tired of insulting the Catholic Church, and I do not at all enjoy in any way this sordid exercise. But I really have no choice on the matter. I have to use shock therapy to deal with such problems like the Church. I have to be cruel in order to be kind.

To continue, by giving limitation to human freedom, the Church is making the unnecessary distinction between freedom and license. The Church says that freedom is not license, which is the irresponsible exercise of freedom. But of course! Nobody disputes that. By making this unnecessary distinction, the Church is unwittingly betraying its ignorance about the distinction between the "essence" of freedom and the "exercise" of freedom. Freedom, in its essence, is the absence of "necessity, coercion, or constraint," as defined by *Merriam-Webster*. In one word, it is absolute. But the exercise of freedom is something else. It cannot be absolute because its exercise necessarily entails the restriction or limitation imposed by the necessity of relative, practical human life. In graphic terms, this means that your freedom to stretch your arm is restricted or limited by the nose of your neighbor. In other words, as a wit puts it, your freedom to extend your arm ends as the nose of your neighbor begins.

But we are not talking about freedom with regard to our neighbor's nose. Our discussion is on freedom vis-à-vis God with regard to sin. On this context, the distinction between the essence and the exercise of freedom is meaningless and irrelevant. With regard to God, you can extend your arm as much as you can without encountering the limitation and restriction of a nose, simply because God has no nose. Although your neighbor cares what you do with your arm in front of his nose, God does not care one way or the other since God gave you the freedom to do what you please with your arm. Of course, what happens in the exercise of your freedom is your own lookout, your own problem, not God's. If in the exercise of your freedom to extend your arm you encounter the problem of a bleeding nose of your neighbor, that is your own problem. And you have to deal with and address your problem by using your head. That is why God gave you your head to solve problems of this sort, among others. But do not be stupid and think that God will punish you for the bleeding nose of your neighbor, as religion taught you. If your neighbor with the bleeding nose return the favor by also giving you a bleeding nose, then you are sufficiently punished. This is simply the law of cause and effect in action. That is all. Nobody punishes you. You punish yourself by the result of your stupid, irresponsible action. You punish yourself by not using your head. So do not again make the stupid mistake of blaming anybody, much less God, for the sufferings you encounter in your life. They are all self-inflicted. God has absolutely nothing to do with it other than making sure that you exercise your freedom. So just blame yourself and gain wisdom for your mistakes so you will not repeat them so that next time, you will exercise your freedom wisely.

In sum, with regard to God, there is no such thing as committing sin because God gave you free will, the ability to do whatever you please, and God will never take that away from you by punishing you in this life or in the next. The real purpose of free will is for you to gain wisdom and, from that wisdom, the ability to evolve in accordance with the universal law of change in order to achieve unlimited perfection.

And so, exorcise from your mind and your system the debilitating and erroneous concept of sin against God together with the stupid idea of hell. They are all erroneous concoction of the error-prone religion. If ever you commit sin, it is not against God but against yourself and your neighbors. It is against yourself for harming yourself. It is against your neighbors for harming them unnecessarily. And who are your neighbors? They are your fellow humans. They are also the animals and plants that give sustenance to our planet and to all its inhabitants including us. They are also the rivers, the seas, the forests, the mountains, the air, that all work together in harmony for the welfare of all creation. These are all our neighbors that we are all enjoined to love as we love ourselves.

In sum, since hell is predicated on the existence of sin, and since there is no sin, it follows that there is also no hell.

Second: Hell vs. God's Intelligence and Goodness

This issue is a mere corollary to the first issue on hell vs. God. Since the first issue has been thoroughly and lengthily addressed, this second one is a forgone conclusion. However, at this juncture, let us embellish our discussion with some poetic insights on the subject from the pen of one of the greatest poets of all times, the one and only Omar Khayyam, a Persian poet, by quoting some relevant verses from his magnum opus, *Rubaiyat*:

"What! Out of senseless nothing to provoke/ A conscious Something to recent the yoke/ Of unpermitted Pleasure, under pain/ Of everlasting Penalties, if broke!

"What! From his helpless creature be repaid/ Pure Gold for what he lent him dross-allay'd/ Sue for a debt he never did contract,/ And cannot answer—Oh, the sorry trade!

"Oh, Thou who didst with pitfall and with Gin/ Beset the Road I was to wander in /Thou wilt not with Predestined Evil round/ Enmesh, and then impute my Fall to Sin.

"Why," said another, "Some there are who tell/ Of One who threatens he will toss to Hell/The luckless Pots he marr'd in making – Pish!/ He's a Good Fellow, and 'twill all be well."

Beautiful, are they not? Indeed, not only beautiful but full of wisdom as well. These verses address perfectly the issue that the religious doctrine of hell is a shocking insult to God's intelligence and goodness. So many people do not realize that they are really insulting God's intelligence and goodness when they believe in the existence of hell. As the poet beautifully said, how can an intelligent Creator blame his creatures for their mistakes when He made them so prone to make mistakes? And why should this intelligent Creator punish his creatures when the latter never asked the former to create them in the first place and there never was a contract between them which the latter can break and thus be punished for breaking it? And lastly, the poet said that the Creator, who placed pitfall and liquor at the road the creature will pass, should not accuse the latter for sinning when he gets drunk and falls into the pitfall nor will the Creator send to hell his creatures He made so imperfect because He is a "Good Fellow" after all and all will be well. Omar Khayyam has given us more proofs for our thesis that sin does not exist.

Third: Hell vs. Survival

Another psychological disease which bedevils humans is insecurity complex. The symptoms of this disease are multifarious. It shows in the humans' deep-seated alienation from their outside world by their unabated destruction of it. It shows in their disconcerting feelings of inadequacy and helplessness that made them do the following: (1) They invent religion together with God and other idols to save them from impending doom beyond their comprehension. (2) They invent the institution of government to assist them in their problems of living with their fellow men. (3) They invent the institution of marriage to give them a sense of stability, completeness, and security in their perceived vagrant, forlorn life. (4) They invent the business of insurance as a hedge against a future they cannot foresee. Indeed, humans' activities and creations cleverly masked their subconscious feelings of inadequacy which is deeply rooted in their natural instinct of survival. In short, humans are not sure of their future. They are not sure of their survival. This is where religion cleverly enters into the picture. Manipulative religion exacerbated this human psychological malady with the fallacious but terribly scary doctrine of hell, which is like the sword of Damocles always hanging over people's heads until they die. Then, after having sufficiently scared humans, religion gives them the good news that there is really no reason to be afraid because religion can save humans from hell if they will do what religion tells them to do. The Catholic Church has perfected this brainwashing technique to such a degree that Catholics are even willing to pay to be its unwitting victims. This technique hides under the name, "retreat." Having attended retreats numerous times during my ignorant religious life, I know but too well what I am talking about. But do not take my word for it. Attend a retreat if you enjoy being thoroughly scared. The priests who conduct retreats have so mastered the art of painting in words how scary hell really is that you will undoubtedly think that they have been to hell and back. The things people do for power and money!

In sum, all these human psychological maladies are caused by the sad failure of humans to find the happiness which their entire being is longing for. They are like lost souls wandering in the wilderness of ignorance in search of their true home. Clever, evil, manipulative religion simply takes advantage of these human psychological maladies by dangling before people's eyes the prospect of religious salvation from hell which is essentially a mere illusion.

This book provides the accurate direction for humans to find happiness and eventually the global peace which is their birthright.

Chapter

19

Marriage and Happiness

Marriage is one of the most difficult subjects one can dare put one's finger into. The reason is the obvious fact that this subject is about the relationship between humans who are individually unique, and therefore, it is like putting a square peg in a round hole, unless you change the configuration of the square peg so that it can fit into the round hole. Knowing this—or perhaps, blissfully oblivious of it—humans, nevertheless, never stop getting married despite the fact that happy or successful marriage is the rare exception rather than the common rule. This means that people enter into a marital relationship thinking, of course, to find heaven on earth or what people call connubial bliss only to find later on that they were sadly mistaken, that the relationship they entered into is more of a hell than anything else. Thus, human life is littered with the debris of countless broken marriages—together, of course, with countless broken hearts. How sad! But so true!

Religion, especially the Catholic religion, compounds this human problem by teaching the wrong dogma that marriage is a relationship that should be permanent. This is definitely a wrong dogma for two obvious reasons: First, we are living in a world where the only permanent is impermanence or change. As Francis Cardinal Newman so beautifully puts it in his tenth sermon, "The Second

Spring": "We have familiar experience of the order, the constancy, the perpetual renovation of the material world which surrounds us. Frail and transitory as is every part of it, restless and migratory as are its elements, never ceasing as are its changes, still it abides... Change upon change—yet one change cries out to another like alternate Seraphim, in praise and in glory of their maker." Since this is so, how then can marriage between two ever-changing people living in an ever-changing world be permanent? Second, human nature is hardwired with the principle that what is forbidden is attractive, a principle whose working we clearly saw in the case of Adam and Eve and the forbidden fruit in the garden of Eden. Has not the Catholic Church learned from that biblical lesson so that the Church has forbidden married people to divorce? Has not the Church thought that by forbidding people to divorce, divorce becomes more attractive, and therefore, people simply rush into it—just like Adam and Eve ate the forbidden fruit when it was forbidden? Thus, the all-knowing Church, by its wrong dogma, adds more fuel to the fire, so to speak, of shattered marriages and bleeding hearts.

Is there no solution to this acute human problem? Is marriage by its very nature inexorably bound with failure and sorrow rather than with success and happiness?

To shed light to this problem, it is imperative that we should have a sufficient understanding of what this conundrum called marriage is all about. We should, therefore, initially define marriage. Unfortunately, the lexicon's definition of marriage adds more energy to this controversy. Let us then engage in a scientific exercise of understanding what marriage is all about by exploring the experience of humans regarding marriage.

History tells us that humans enter into a marital relationship for so many reasons that have nothing to do with sexual intercourse. But in general, humans marry for sexual union—as the Bible says: "Therefore, a man shall leave his father and mother and be joined to his wife, and they shall become one flesh" (Genesis 2:24). The essence of marriage, therefore, is the agreement of a man and a woman to live together as husband and wife, which, of course, involves sexual intercourse, as the Bible says. That is the traditional definition of marriage. However, times and people have changed, and consequently, tradition has also changed so that today marriage, which traditionally is a union between a man and a woman, is now simply a union between consenting adults without any gender requirement. Thus, same-sex marriage is now legally recognized in many first world countries including the United States because of numerous couples of the same sex living together in marital union.

That said, it still remains a sad fact that broken marriage is still the social norm rather than the exception. Broken marriage, in this context, means the parties to the marriage are unhappy about the union and therefore either physically or emotionally separate from one another or both. Thus, legal separation, annulment of marriage, divorce, and de-facto separation—any of these are availed of by the unhappy couples or they just live together in one roof but not as husbands and wives.

It would seem, therefore, that in general, happiness is not an essential part of marriage. Since this is so, what is the secret of those rare happily married couple? Their secret is not really a secret. Anyone can read it in their happy faces. Their happy faces reveal the fact that their personal happiness is the cause of their happy marriage. In other words, they are happily married because they are happy. In other words, these happily married couples are in themselves individually happy, and it does not make any difference to their happiness if their marriage is a success or not. And the happy result is that since they are happy, willy-nilly, their marriage is also happy as a result of their being happy. In short, their happy marriage is the effect of their being happy. The principle at work here is: our life is simply a mirror of ourselves. Thus, if we want to have a happy marriage or, for that matter, a happy life, we have to be happy. Thus, the numerous unhappy marriages in this world speaks volumes of the huge number of unhappy people.

This brings us to the supreme significance of the principle of happiness.

Before we go to the important next chapter, we have to emphasize the fact that the real cause of unhappy marriage is the fact that the parties to the marriage are unhappy people. Since they are unhappy people, whatever relationships they enter into— whether marriage, employment, friendship, etc.—are bound to be unhappy by virtue of the principle: the nature of the effect is the nature of the cause. Jesus Christ, the supreme teacher, expressed this all-important principle in these graphic terms: "Even so, every good tree bears good fruit, but a bad tree bears bad fruit. A good tree cannot bear bad fruit, nor can a bad tree bear good fruit... Therefore, by their fruits you shall know them" (Matthew 7:17–20).

Needless to say, unhappily married people should be guided by this essential principle of life, if they want to have a happy marriage. There are many lessons that one can reap from the above discussion. First and foremost is that relationship is a difficult undertaking in life and the most difficult one is that of marriage. One, therefore, should not jump into marriage if one is not ready for it. Second, one should not enter into a marital relationship with the desire to get happiness from it. If that is your motivation, then you are not ready for marriage, and if you still marry, then you will surely be disappointed because nobody gets happiness from marriage. Rather, your motivation for marrying should be to give happiness or to share your happiness to your partner. Then you are ready for marriage. Then your happiness will be enhanced or multiplied, if you will, and your marriage will be a success. Third, before you get married, make sure that you are already happy so you can give or share your happiness to your loved one. Remember that no one gives what he does not have. Fourth, since marriage per se does not and will not give you happiness but simply enhances or multiplies your happiness, you are not compelled by nature to marry. This is one area in life where you can exercise your God-given freedom since it has nothing to do with your basic need for happiness. Hence, you may or may not marry depending on your choice, values, or inclination. Do not be affected by social pressure that you should get married. Those people who are pressuring others to marry are simply acting on the principle that misery loves company.

Fifth, if you get married, remember this: marital relationship, like everything else in this changeable life, is subject to change. Your married life might be a rose garden, but that rose garden is subject to the vagaries of the four seasons. Be prepared, therefore, for the changes that the four seasons of life will bring to your marriage. It does not mean that your marriage is an unhappy one or a failure, if now and then you quarrel with your wife or you experience some unavoidable tragedy in your married life. It only means that, as the French say, "C'est la vie" (Such is life) and your married life is no exception to life in general. Always remember that in this relative world we live in, there is no joy without pain, there is no day without night, there is no happiness without sorrow.

During the stormy time of life, be a stable unsinkable ship and you can only be one if you are happy.

Chapter

20

Divorce and Happiness

Like marriage, divorce is also a difficult subject to understand, let alone discuss. The reason for this is not really the subject itself, but the huge controversy surrounding it. Divorce is one subject which divides the whole world. The libertarians are for divorce, for obvious reasons. The conservatives—religious conservatives, that is, especially religious fundamentalists—are against it. The religion which is leading the fight against divorce is none other than the "great" Catholic church whose numerous members are literally legions compared to the other religions. In some Catholic countries, like the Philippines, the fight against divorce led by the Catholic Church has taken such a proportion and intensity that politicians are unable to pass a bill legalizing divorce. Hence, in the Philippines, couples who are desperate to separate have to resort to a very expensive, tedious, and lengthy legal process called annulment of marriage. Thus, those who cannot afford to go through this legal process either resort to de-facto separation or simply suffer the misery of living in an unhappy marriage until death releases them from their agony.

In this chapter, we will not go through the misery and agony of unraveling the legal or moral mystery of divorce. We will simply stick to our theme of happiness and discuss the relevance of divorce to human happiness.

To be happy, one must first be not unhappy. Therefore, if something is making you unhappy, you must first remove that something so that you can be not unhappy. Then you can start working on being happy. Hence, if your marriage is making you unhappy, then by all means, get rid of your marriage by getting a divorce. However, a word of caveat. This is easier said than done. Divorce, as you know is not an ordinary action, like walking, which has practically no consequence. Divorce is a crucial action which has significant consequences in your life that are difficult to predict. These significant consequences might redound either to your benefit or to your disaster. Whichever way the cookie crumbles, as the saying goes, you can never be sure of. For all you know, you might be jumping from one frying pan to another, to use another cliché. And for all you know, the other frying pan might be a hotter one. This underscores the critical significance not only of getting divorce, but of getting married as well—because were it not for marriage, you would not have to divorce. The point is: be always extra careful in what you do, especially if what you do is as important in your life as marriage and divorce.

But then, life in general is a gamble and marriage is one of the biggest and dangerous gamble of all. Hence, if you are a gambler and you gamble your happiness by getting married and lost the gamble, then be more careful this time when you think of betting on divorce. You might develop the bad habit of losing. And that will not be good for your happiness.

Chapter

21

The Principle of Vacuum and Happiness

In the chapter on the meaning of happiness, we defined happiness in terms of physics as a vacuum in a human system filled. However, we did not elaborate on this definition of happiness culled from the principle of physics regarding vacuum. But since the importance of the dynamics of the principle of vacuum vis- à-vis happiness cannot be overstated, this book on happiness will not be complete without a thorough discussion of the relationship between the principle of vacuum and the principle of happiness.

At the outset, it should be made clear that the principle of happiness is simply an extension of the principle of vacuum. Why? Because the principle of vacuum permeates not only the physical realm (physics)[44] but also the mental and spiritual realm. And the other side of the equation of this principle of vacuum is the principle that nature abhors vacuum, and therefore, vacuum should be filled to satisfy nature. Now, in terms of the human dynamics of happiness, vacuum is simply the unfulfilled needs of humans in his physical, mental, and spiritual components. Happiness, therefore, for humans simply consists in fulfilling these human needs which are actually vacuums or vacua in the human system.

Now, what is exactly a vacuum, and why does nature abhor vacuum? Vacuum is best defined by one word: emptiness or void. Nature, however, according to the lexicon, is the "world in its entirety." In one word, therefore, nature is totality or fullness. In this sense, nature is the opposite of vacuum. And vacuum is the "enemy" of nature, if you will. That is why nature abhors vacuum because vacuum is nature's enemy—in the sense that emptiness is the enemy of fullness. Since nature (fullness) abhors vacuum (emptiness), wherever there is a vacuum, nature does everything in its power to eliminate it by filling it up with its fullness. Hence, "fulfillment" essentially means nature doing what it likes best: filling up emptiness with its fullness.

However, in the realm of human domain, nature is not always successful in filling up the numerous vacuums in man's being. Why? Because nature is impeded either by human ignorance or by human will or both. Hence, unfortunately for nature or humans or both, it is only in the human realm that nature cannot fully exercise its power because humans have also their own willpower which can impede or counteract nature's will. Nevertheless, when nature's will of filling up the vacuums in man's being is impeded by humans, nature does not give up easily. In fact, it never gives up. This results in a natural war in man's being—a war between man and nature that lasts until nature wins. It is this war which is the cause of man's unhappiness. Sad to say, there are numerous victims of this still ongoing war.

Now, what is the moral lesson in the above story of war between humans and nature? If you are unhappy, you can be sure that there is a vacuum in your being, a vacuum demanding to be filled causing your unhappiness What to do? In the light of the natural principles discussed in this book, make a self-examination. Search every nook and cranny of your being and look for any need which is not fulfilled and fill it up right away in accordance with the principles previously discussed. That is the only way to end up the natural war within you. That is the only way to be happy. For instance, if you are lonely and therefore unhappy, that is a sure symptom that there is a vacuum in your being demanding to be filled. That vacuum may be the fact that your spiritual need is not fulfilled. Hence, simply fulfill your spiritual need by the practice of transcendental meditation so you can establish a proper relationship with the absolute component of your being, a relationship which your spirit needs.

Another symptom or telltale sign that you have a vacuum in your system or being is when you have an abnormal or compulsive desire for something like food, for instance, which you cannot control. You can be sure that your abnormal and compulsive desire for food is nature's way of telling you that you have a vacuum in your system or in any components of your being—the physical, mental, and spiritual—which you are trying to fill up incorrectly by overeating. The solution therefore is to discover that vacuum and fill it up accordingly and correctly. You can do this by self-examination, as previously mentioned, or by consulting a psychiatrist to help you understand your problem.

Human society is replete of examples of individuals who are victims of maladies stemming from the vacuum principle. An obvious example consists of those who are deprived of their need for sex or love or both. To this group belong those obese spinsters, nuns, and priests who subconsciously attempt to fill up the void in their being by overeating. Pedophile priests also belong to this unfortunate group. These poor priests do not realize that their sexual aberration stems from their futile attempts to cover up the deprivation of their natural need for normal sex.

Another not so obvious example because they are so common are people who live empty lives. They might be wallowing in material wealth, but their minds and their souls are empty. Consequently, they are really the poorest on earth. In accordance with the natural principle of the vacuum, they try to cover up this emptiness in their lives by material things. They spend all their empty lives accumulating material possessions like big house, the latest car, expensive clothes and glittering jewelries they adorn their bodies with, and on, and on, and on. Their passion for material things is endless, not knowing that their abnormal obsession is simply the symptom of the huge emptiness in their being. At the end of the day, these poor souls leave this earth wondering what happened to their useless, empty lives. What a tragedy!

Another example consists of those unhappy individuals who are victims of drugs (alcohol, tobacco, cannabis, cocaine, etc.) that they use as dangerous substitutes to fill up their lack of happiness. Speaking of drugs, the vicar of St. George Episcopal Church in Hawthorne, California, Rev. Leo Booth, in his groundbreaking book, *When God Becomes a Drug*, defended the thesis that religion can be a drug and that addiction caused by religion is a disease which can be treated like alcohol addiction. (This is another compelling argument against the existence of religion.) Anyway, whatever kind of drug may be the cause of addiction, the only cure for it is to realize that addiction is only a symptom, a surface manifestation that deep inside the being of the addict, there is a huge vacuum demanding to be filled, and unless that demand is addressed satisfactorily, the symptom will continue to manifest to the detriment of the individual addict.

Speaking of addiction, people do not realize that they can also be addicted to delicious but harmful foods like meat and other junk foods that cause deadly and painful diseases like cancer, diabetes, cardiovascular problems, arthritis, etc. Their addiction has deteriorated to such an extent that instead of eating in order to live, they live in order to eat. Unfortunately, they do not live long enough to enjoy their addiction. The people who are victims of this kind of addiction also do not realize that they are actually committing suicide because although they are slowly killing themselves, nevertheless, they are surely killing themselves, which is the definition of suicide.45 To this type of addiction, the same principle of the ubiquitous vacuum applies as its only cure.

Indeed, the principle of the vacuum is so intimately connected with human happiness that if you feel unhappy, you can reasonably suspect that there is a vacuum within your being demanding to be filled. And fill it you must to regain your happiness.

If you are happy and you multiply yourself sufficiently, then there will be finally peace on earth.

Chapter

22

The Meaning and Purpose of Life and Existence

Now that you know the nature of happiness and how to achieve it, what then? Have you now achieved the purpose of life, your own life? Have you now found the meaning of existence, your own existence? This book will not be complete without addressing these fundamental issues about life and existence, including God's existence which is inextricably linked with human life and existence. Oh yes, let us try to do the impossible: inquire about the purpose of the ultimate existence. If we can find the answer to this supreme enigma, then we can also find the answer to the equally enigmatic purpose of human existence. But how are we going to do this? How can we look behind the mysterious veil that separates the relative realm from the absolute? There is really no need to do that since reality is one and seamless. All we have to do then is to apply the hermetic principle of correspondence: as above, so below. It is called hermetic because it was formulated by Hermes Trismegistus, the legendary author of the esoteric principles of the universe.

Let us then start from the supreme being. Since God is all-perfect, it follows that God is the happiest being there is. If so, why did God create the universe? Is it not enough for God to be perfectly happy so that he triggers the big bang of creation? Is not the state of being perfectly happy the purpose and meaning of God's existence? The fact that God, despite being perfectly happy, created the universe and continues the act of creation without letup tells us that perfect happiness is not the be-all and end-all of God's existence. It tells us that the meaning and purpose of God's existence is found not in happiness but in creation. But why creation? What is in creation that gives meaning and purpose to God's existence? As we shall shortly see, the ultimate answer to this ultimate question is experience.

Despite the mind-boggling infinite numbers of the disparate objects of creation, there is one denominator common to them all: experience. It is experience which everything in creation is doing. Even if they are not doing anything, even that is experience. But what does experience have to do with God? Everything! Despite all the inconceivable perfections God possesses, there is still something which his absolute being prevents him from having. That something, which only relative beings have, is experience: the result of interactions between beings. But since God is absolute and there can only be one absolute being, God has nobody with whom he can interact. Hence, God cannot have experience. Without experience, which gives God knowledge of other beings apart from himself, it is as if God does not exist at all since there is nobody with whom he can relate and compare himself with and appreciate his own being. Hence, God has to create the universe. In this sense, it can truly be said that God created the universe and the universe created God.[46]

Since experience is the factor which gives meaning and purpose to God's existence, the same is true for all created beings. The same is true for humans. As above, so below. Hence, stripped of any religious, philosophical, and scientific trappings, experience is the answer to life's purpose. And since to experience life is nothing more than to live life, the purpose of life is simply to live life. But are we really living life? Or do we just go through life half-awake or half-asleep? When Jesus said, "Father, forgive them for they do not know what they are doing," is he not referring to the whole of humanity who are not fully conscious of what they are doing, and therefore in reality, they really do not know what they are doing, which explains why they are making so many mistakes like crucifying Jesus? Has not Jesus, by those words, spelled out the real problem of humans: that they are not living properly and therefore not only missing out on life, but also making life a mess? The answer is found implicitly in the aforementioned words of Jesus: we have to know what we are doing. In other words, we have to be fully conscious every moment we are awake. Jesus, in effect, was saying that our presence should be complete in whatever we are doing so that we do not miss anything in life. So we should not allow our mind to snatch our consciousness from the present and hold it hostage to the past or the future. If we allow our mind to do this, then we are not really living life because life happens in the present and not in the past nor in the future. Then we miss out on life. Then we have not experienced reality. Then we are a failure to ourselves. We are a failure to the universe. We are a failure to God.

Hence, to live life fully is to be fully aware, to be fully conscious every waking moment of our life with our body, mind, and spirit. To live life fully is to interact with our environment, with the world, in the fullness of our being. To live life fully is to surrender our being to the being of the present.

In sum, the meaning or purpose of human life and existence is simply to experience life fully. It does not really matter what we experience. What matters is how we experience it. It does not really matter what kind of life we live because we are destined to live all kinds of lives. What matters is whether we have truly experienced that life. In the final analysis, experience is the only reason for living. And an integral part of this experience is to experience happiness.

Our experience of happiness should not be complete without the experience of peace on earth.

CONCLUSION

To recapitulate, the following are the salient points of our thesis worth noting:

1. Happiness is simply the fulfillment or satisfaction of the basic needs of humans.
2. The basic needs of humans pertain to the needs of the three basic components of their being, namely: body, mind, and spirit taken as a whole
3. Hence, happiness consists of the holistic or integral fulfillment of the needs of the human body, mind, and spirit taken as one, which is the meaning of "holistic" and "integral."
4. Happiness and holiness are one and the same thing since holiness is also the holistic fulfillment of the needs of the triune components of man's being consisting of the physical, mental, and spiritual. Hence, if one is truly happy, one is also truly holy and vice versa. Conversely, if one is not truly happy, one is also not truly holy and vice versa.
5. Happiness can be found and achieved in this life since all the ingredients of happiness exist in this life. Hence, one can be truly happy in this life and does not have to wait for the afterlife to find happiness. If you subscribe to the erroneous religious teaching that happiness can be found only in heaven after you die, then you are a sorry victim of religion and your life on earth is totally wasted.
6. Happiness, like perfection, has many degrees. The challenge of life is to be able to achieve the ultimate happiness. This is the dynamics of human evolution which can all happen and must happen in this earthly life of humans. Humans are

destined to achieve and enjoy the ultimate perfection which includes happiness.

7. Consciousness and happiness are intimately related since we experience happiness through our consciousness. Consciousness like happiness has many degrees. The ultimate challenge of life is to achieve the supreme consciousness which is unity consciousness.

8. The principle of the vacuum and happiness are intimately related. If you are unhappy, see if you have an unfilled vacuum within yourself, and if so, lose no time in addressing it completely and properly, not by accumulating useless material things to cover your emptiness.

9. The meaning and purpose of life is to experience life, to live life fully by being fully conscious of the present. Happiness is an integral component of this experience.

10. Happiness is the only key to peace on earth.

That, in so many words, is the philosophy of happiness. It is the philosophy of sorrow, agony, and pain because happiness is inextricably bound with all of them. It is the philosophy of human history because happiness and sorrow are the colorful warp and woof of the never-ending beautiful tapestry of human history. It is the philosophy of every man, woman, and child because their lives and existence are the precious materials that make up the exciting drama of human destiny. It is the philosophy of God and his creation since they consist of the matrix and substance that are the sine quibus non of happiness. Indeed, it is the philosophy of life itself with all its joys, sorrows, and pain.

It is also the philosophy of war and peace. As we saw, without war, there can be no peace, and without peace, there can be no war. But the problem is, there is too much war and hardly is there peace. As I wrote in one of my books, we live in a cruel world where violence is the staple of life and peace is only a beautiful dream. The world is besieged with never-ending conflicts among nations and among the people within the nations. This is the dark bloody picture which history has always been showing about the world. It is not a portrait of war and peace but a chiaroscuro of wars interspersed with peace, only to highlight the gloomy colors of war.

It is time that peace should reign in the world if only so we can enjoy and appreciate the excitement of war, the glorious victory of having triumphed in a marvelous war, the awesome feeling of having forgiven and assisted with magnanimity the fallen enemy. We are missing all these wondrous blessings of war because of the absence of peace. We have been living too long with the culture of war and death that we have been immune to them. We should therefore do something to bring peace to our war-weary life. The only way to do this is also to bring happiness to our sorrow-weary souls. The world is only a mirror of ourselves. If we are not happy, the world will always be at war. Our being creates our world. If we are miserable, our world will always suffer the misery of war. If we are happy, the world will be at peace.

Hence, the importance of being happy, the imperative necessity of human happiness, and the crucial significance of this book. Hence, I hope and I wish that having read this book, you come to the conclusion and conviction that if there is a book you need to have and keep all your life and keep on reading over and over again, it is this book. Indeed, if there is any knowledge you need in order to have a happy and successful life, it is in this book. But knowledge without wisdom, which is knowledge put into practice, is useless or, at best, only a mere ego booster. Therefore, after reading this book, the best and wise thing you should do is to think of effective ways and means to put into practice the precious knowledge you acquired and to share it with your friends and other loved ones.

A philosophical opus, like this book, is normally a difficult reading material. Philosophers have the wrong notion that philosophy should be abstruse and incomprehensible. So they develop the bad habit of producing so-called philosophical writings that are also abstruse and incomprehensible. I have a strong suspicion that they do not really know what they are writing about so that they are compelled to violate the cardinal principle of writing: clarity. Anyway, most of their writings are hogwash and have no bearing to human life. Hence, it does not really matter if they are incomprehensible. But this philosophic book is about the most fundamental element of human life: happiness. Hence, I made sure—painstakingly—that any intelligent and literate human like yourself will have no trouble in trying to understand its all-important message and implement it in your life so that if you multiply yourself sufficiently, my number one obsession will finally be fulfilled. As you already know, that obsession is peace on earth.

With the present state of the world, where many people drink violence as their coffee for breakfast and eat bullets as their main course for dinner, my obsession for world peace is getting more and more acute while the prospect of its being realized is getting more and more to be an impossible dream.

However, since "Impossible Dream" is one of the songs I love to sing, peace on earth is also one of the obsessions I love to fantasize about, hoping against hope that one beautiful day, the dark cloud of insanity will finally disperse and the bright light of reason will come through and enlighten people's minds and flood it with the blissful joy of peace.

Happiness and peace be with you and with the whole universe!

BIBLIOGRAPHY

Almeder, R. *Human Happiness and Morality*. Buffalo, N.Y.: Prometheus Press, 2008.

Annas, J. *The Morality of Happiness*. New York: Oxford, 1993.

Argyle, M. The *Psychology of Happiness*. New York: Routledge, 2002.

Bainton, R. H. The Medieval Church. New York: Van Nostrand, 1962. Burnet, J. *Early Greek Philosophy*. 4th ed. London: Black, 1930.

Bruteau, B. *Evolution Toward Divinity*. Wheaton IL: Theosophical Publishing House, 1974.

Cahn, S. M. and Vitrano, C. *Happiness: Classical and Contemporary Readings in Philosophy*. New York: Oxford, 2008.

Checola, M. "Happiness, Rationality, Autonomy and the Good Life." *Journal of Happiness Studies*, 8(1): 51–78, 2007.

Copleston, Frederick. *Thomas Aquinas*. New York: Harper and Row, 1955.

Corpus, A. *The Spiritual and Ethical Dimension of Vegetarianism*. U.S.A.: Xlibris LLC, 2014.

Davis, W. "Pleasure and Happiness." *Philosophical Studies*, 39: 305–318, 1981.

Diener, E. and Seligman, M. "Beyond Money: Toward an Economy of Well-Being." *Psychological Science in the Public Interest*, 5(1): 1–31, 2004.

Eliot, T. S., *The Wasteland and Other Poems*. New York: Buccaneer Books, 1958.

Feldman, F. *Pleasure and the Good Life*. New York: Oxford, 2004. Findlay, J. N. *Plato and Platonism*. New York: Times Books, 1978. Frey, B. S. *Happiness: A Revolution in Economics*. Cambridge, MA: MIT Press, 2008.

Guthrie, W. K. C. *Greek Philosophy*. London: Methuen, 1950.

The Holy Bible. New King James Version. Giant Print Edition. Thomas Nelson Publisher, 1982.

Hurka, T. *The Best Things in Life: A Guide to What Really Matters.* New York: Oxford University Press, 2010.

Kant, Immanuel. *Groundwork of the Metaphysics of Morals*. Edited and translated by Allen W. Wood. New Haven and London: Yale University Press, 2002.

Krishnamurti, J. *The First and Last Freedom*. India: Krishnamurti Foundation, 1998.

Layard, R. *Happiness: Lessons from a New Science*. New York: Penguin, 2005.

Lyubomirsky, S. *The How of Happiness*. New York: Penguin, 2007. McMahon, D. M. *Happiness: A History*. Atlantic Monthly Press, 2005. Mayerfeld, J. "The Moral Asymmetry of Happiness and Suffering."

Southern Journal of Philosophy, 34: 317–315.

More, Thomas. *Utopia*. New Haven and London: Yale University Press, 1964.

Myers, D. G. *Theories of Emotion*. Psychology: Seventh Edition. New York, NY: Worth Publishers, 2004.

Nietzsche, F., *Thus Spoke Zarathustra*. Walter Kaufmann (trans.), New York: Penguin Books, 1958.

Noddings, N. *Happiness and Education*. New York: Cambridge University Press, 2003.

Rawls, J. *A Theory of Justice*. Cambridge, MA: Harvard University Press, 1971.

Rawlings, M. *Beyond Death's Door*. New York: Bantam Books, 1978. Raz, J. "The Role of Well Being." *Philosophical Perspectives*, 18(1): 269–294, 2004.

The Holy Quran. Translated by Maulana Muhammad Ali. Ohio, U.S.A.: Ahmadiyya Anjuman Isha'at Islam Lahore Inc., 2002.

Schacht, R. *Nietzsche*. London: Routledge, 1983.

Scruton, R. *Reason and Happiness: Nature and Conduct*. R. S. Peters (ed.) New York: MacMillan 139–61, 1975.

Smith, H. *The Religions of Man*. New York: Harper and Row, 1958.
Solomon, R. and Higgins, K. *A Short History of Philosophy*, New York: Oxford University Press, 1996.

Sukkanen, J. "An Improved Whole Life Satisfaction Theory of Happiness." *International Journal of Wellbeing*, 1(1): 1–18, 2011.

Tatarkiewicz, W. *Analysis of Happiness*. The Hague: Martinus Nijhof, 1976.

Taylor, Alfred E. *Aristotle*. Mineola, N.Y. Dover, 1955.

Whitehead, Alfred North. *Adventures of Ideas*. New York: Macmillan, 1933.

Williams, O. (ed.) *Immortal Poems of the English Language*. Washington Square Press: New York, 1952.

ENDNOTES

1. The best thing this intellectual giant could come up with regarding happiness was the word "eudaemonia," which means "the good life."
2. *The Spiritual and Ethical Dimension of Vegetarianism*
3. *The Philosophy of LGBT*
4. Buddha was not only young but totally inexperienced regarding the facts of life, having been raised by his father within the confines of his luxurious palace.
5. This incident I find remarkably un-Christlike and does not speak well of Christ's intelligence. Why hurt an innocent tree whose time for bearing fruit has not yet come? This I find absolutely shocking, to say the least!
6. This account on Socrates is taken from Wikipedia.
7. Ibid.
8. This account on Aristotle is partly taken from Wikipedia.
9. Ibid.
10. Ibid.
11. Ibid.
12. *Summa Theologiae*, Part 2, Q.1, Article 8
13. Wikipedia, ibid.
14. Wikipedia, ibid.
15. Wikipedia, ibid.
16. Wikipedia, ibid.
17. Op. cit.
18. Op. cit.
19. I submit that this is the proper and right definition of man. Aristotle's definition of man as a rational animal is therefore incomplete.

20. Religions of Man, ibid. p.

21. Amazon and the other major book outlets carry these two books.

22. *Merriam-Webster*, Ibid. p.1299

23. J. Krishnamurti. *The First and Last Freedom*. (India: Krishnamurti Foundation, 1998) 19.

24. To understand the Bible, especially the first five books of the Old Testament called the Pentateuch, one should read Zecharia Sitchin's *The 12ᵗʰ Planet*.

25. This is the teaching of Maharishi Mahesh Yogi, the famous guru of the Beatles, to which this writer subscribes.

26. William Wordsworth, *Immortal Poems of the English Language*, Oscar Williams, (ed.), New York: Washington Square Press, 1952, p.260.

27. William Blake, Ibid., p.235.

28. Huston Smith, *Religions of Man*.

29. The original words of Shakespeare are: "There are more in heaven and earth, Horatio, than are dreamt of in your philosophy."

30. *Merriam-Webster's Collegiate Dictionary*, Eleventh Edition, p.691.

31. This is not the only advantage of empirical knowledge. It is also the only knowledge of which the knower can really be sure of because it is based and culled from his personal experience.

32. The tabula rasa doctrine of John Locke does not square with human experience, particularly with the existence of child prodigies.

33. It is, of course, obvious that it is not possible to achieve perfection in just one lifetime. Thus, when Christ said, "Be ye perfect as the heavenly Father is perfect," he assumed the existence of reincarnation.

34. Ibid. p.1140.

35. Friedrich Nietzsche, *Thus Spoke Zarathustra*, Walter Kaufman (trans.), New York: Penguin Books, 1978, p. 55.

36. Ibid. p. 66.

37. This is also called the evolutionary theory of emotion.

38. T. S. Eliot, *The Wasteland and Other Poems*. New York: Buccaneer Books,1958, p.20.

39. This principle is graphically exemplified by the story of Adam and Eve violating the injunction not to eat the so-called forbidden fruit.

40. Why God did not use this type of persuasion in the case of Adam and Eve is beyond me.

41. Compare this philosophy with that of Thomas More enunciated in his book *Utopia* where he said that money itself is the root of all evils. Thus, he went on to design an ideal economic system where money does not exist and is not needed.

42. In the case of Job, the Bible says that "the Lord gave Job twice as much as he had before" after Job has successfully borne his sufferings (Job 12:10). In terms of evolution, this means that Job's successful struggle against the problems of his life resulted in his acquiring a superior state of life.

43. Koran 2:24.

44. The principle of vacuum in physics is best and commonly exemplified by the gadget siphon.

45. What is a huge mystery for me is the fact that the religious people who commit this kind of suicide do not consider it a sin. For them, what is sinful is when you kill yourself not slowly but quickly like hanging yourself or putting a bullet in your head. But when you kill yourself slowly by smoking or by eating meat, that is absolutely OK.

46. For those who espouse the position that God created the universe from his own substance and therefore the universe is also divine, this whole idea or process of God creating the universe is God playing with himself, a pure make-believe. Thus, it can be said that reality is a game, a divine game.

www.ingramcontent.com/pod-product-compliance
Lightning Source LLC
Chambersburg PA
CBHW051524120626
46551CB00012B/1061